FRENCH FOOD SAFARI

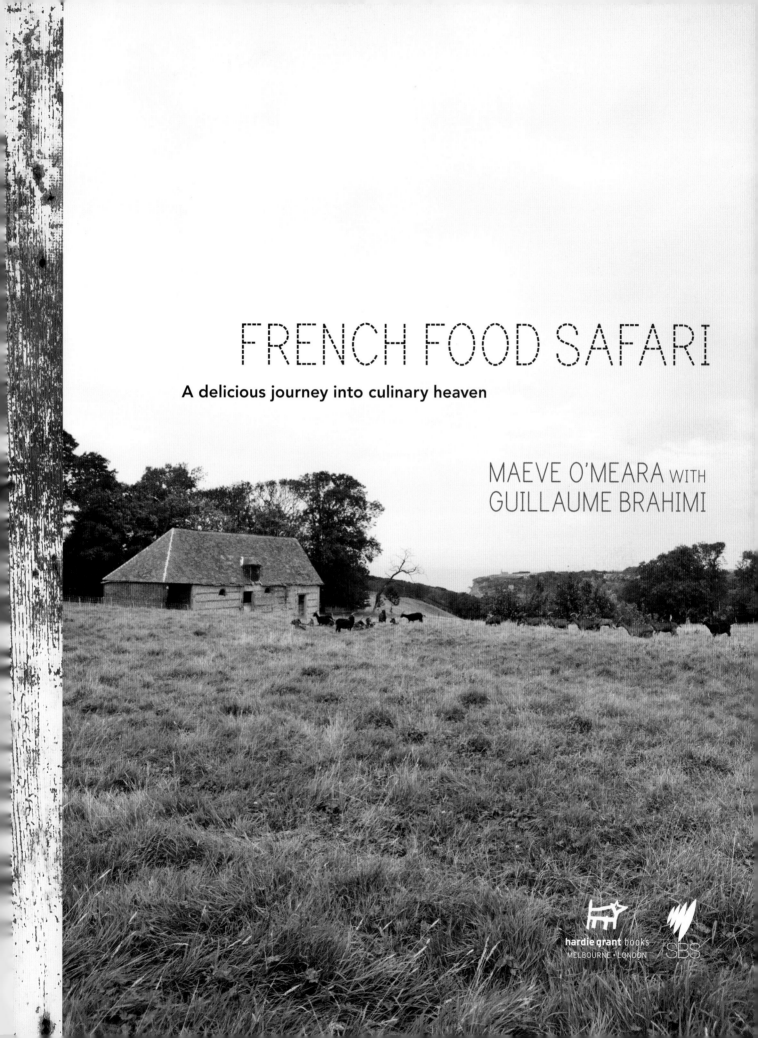

FRENCH FOOD SAFARI

A delicious journey into culinary heaven

MAEVE O'MEARA WITH
GUILLAUME BRAHIMI

hardie grant books
MELBOURNE · LONDON

SBS

CONTENTS

INTRODUCTION

The French have it all – oceans of style in every part of their lives from fashion to food. It seems effortless, and in a sense it is. The French grow up *knowing* the season for scallops and asparagus; how to choose an artichoke; what a roast chicken should really taste like; and that cheese always comes before dessert. The sheer joy, the exquisite pleasure of eating French-style, is simply a part of life.

This book of recipes aims to give you some of the essence of French culture and cuisine – a window into the French world. It is based on the television series *French Food Safari*, which explored the best of French food in France and Australia, spending time with top chefs as well as in warm home kitchens.

The timing of our filming in France was fortuitous as we were in the kitchen of one of the masters – the very charming Guy Savoy who has Michelin-starred restaurants around the world – when the announcement came through that the United Nations Educational, Scientific and Cultural Organisation (UNESCO) had decreed the French meal one of the 'intangible cultural treasures' of the world, officially honouring the way the French value food, wine, and meal times with family and friends.

Savoy was one of the chefs who joined the French president to push for this acknowledgement, and so we all celebrated – with his signature oysters, freshly shucked and served with a marvellous iced oyster aspic that had a hint of sorrel, pepper and tiny shards of lemon. These were served with a glass of Champagne, because you must celebrate with food and wine – *bien sûr* ('of course')! This to many of us is civilisation at its absolute best.

Other countries have similar traditions, but the French have 'a certain marriage of foods and wines, a succession of dishes, a way of sitting down for a meal and talking about it, that is specifically French' – those are the words of Jean-Robert Pitte who was head of the group that approached UNESCO. He's right about the almost forensic focus on food in France – you've never heard such high-grade food conversation as the French discussing what they've just eaten and what they're planning for tonight's dinner.

Here is a whole nation that eagerly awaits the first luscious wild strawberry of the season, the first white asparagus or basket of morels fresh from the forest; who shudder at the thought of a baguette over two hours old; and who will walk

miles to the best purveyor of seafood or charcuterie simply because their tastebuds demand it. Here is a nation that treasures its food and wine with an almost religious fervour.

Renowned chef Guillaume Brahimi accompanied us on our travels, our guide to the intricacies of the French world. He trained in France in some of the top kitchens, including that of exacting master Joël Robuchon. Guillaume now has restaurants in Sydney, Melbourne and Perth and is a wonderful ambassador for the place of his birth.

Throughout our travels in France, Guillaume had a favourite word – 'respect'. It was used by producers to talk about their work; by chefs to talk about produce; and by providores in referring to how they looked after their customers. 'Aha!' Guillaume said when spending time below the streets of Paris in the fragrant cheese-rooms of Laurent Dubois, top *affineur* (cheese ripener and seller), and again in the warm kitchen of pâtissier Fabrice le Bourdat. 'There's that word again! Everyone who really knows food talks about respect.'

The French have a true respect for food that is seen in the care taken to grow, raise and create food, as well as in the care taken to shop for and select the best food to eat. It's referred to as *l'art de vivre* – 'the art of living', which is taught from an early age according to Guillaume.

'From the simple things like shopping for bread three times a day, going to one *fromager* for your goat's cheese and another for your brie because each one has a different speciality – we grow up with this, it's our way of life,' he says.

Many of us know the similar phrase *joie de vivre* – 'the joy of living', a phrase that captures the French spirit of living in the moment, enjoying everything from conversation to food. This is the spirit we hope inspires you in this book of recipes from so many talented people – a guide to some of the best food in the world.

'AS FAR AS CUISINE IS CONCERNED ONE MUST READ EVERYTHING, SEE EVERYTHING, HEAR EVERYTHING, TRY EVERYTHING, OBSERVE EVERYTHING, IN ORDER TO RETAIN IN THE END, JUST A LITTLE BIT.'
Fernand Point, 20th century chef and restaurateur

THE VILLAGE

THE VILLAGE

France is renowned for its high-end, modern gastronomy and complex dishes, but there is another side to French life – in the countryside, the village and the average home where food is more rustic and traditional. It follows the seasons and generally features what is available in the region. The food is not fussy but nourishing and delicious, and perfected by generations of home cooks. This is where classic French dishes like cassoulet, coq au vin, beef bourguignon and lamb navarin have come from, along with beautifully simple recipes like *crique Ardèchois*.

One home kitchen we were lucky enough to be invited into was that of best-selling cookbook author and chef Stéphane Reynaud, who lives with his family in the village of Saint-Agrève in the mountainous area of the Ardèche in south-east France. He's a firm believer that the soul of French cooking is in the home and in the regions of France. He has a restaurant in Paris and commutes each week from the village. It's a place where he finds solace and inspiration, and where he delights in getting back to basics like curing his own *jambon sec* (air-dried ham) using wild herbs and pine needles, making butter, and spending afternoons with family and friends.

The weekend we visited, Stéphane was rallying the troops to make a regional speciality – *saucisse de couenne*. This is a rustic sausage made with coarsely minced (ground) pork flavoured with smoky pork skin and fat that is roasted over a fire of pinecones. It was a glorious moment joining Stéphane as everyone, especially the kids, got into roasting the pork skin and later piping out the delicious sausages. They were baked and savoured with a couple of good bottles of wine from Stéphane's extensive underground cellar, plus a cheese board the size of a cart wheel with fifteen different cheeses and some wonderful sourdough. And that was just for starters!

In the warm, open-plan kitchen a huge pot-au-feu was scenting the air, and the atmosphere combined with the tantalising aromas made us feel we had tapped into the essence of French life. It was totally food-centric, but in the most unpretentious way. Stéphane was incredibly generous to let a film crew into his home for a day, and it added up to one of the great days of our lives.

Like Stéphane curing his own ham, there can be a lot of DIY surrounding life in the country. Some of the joys of being outside a city include the ability to grow some of what you eat, whether fruit, vegetables or herbs; keep chickens and other animals; and, depending on the region, forage for wild food in the forests, along the shoreline, or in the local rivers and streams. The essence of country life is to make the most of what's available, and to waste nothing – and why would you when cep or chanterelle mushrooms await you in the forest, plums are blushing on the trees, or there are wild snails to gather for a feast?

Dany Chouet introduced many Australians to French food at her restaurants in Sydney and the Blue Mountains and now lives in Périgord in south-west France. She revels in the different foods of each season, including ripe summer tomatoes, plump prunes from nearby Agen that are a year-round staple, and a more unusual regional delight – the lamprey. This unique freshwater fish is often likened to a baby eel and has a short season in spring. 'When the lamprey come up the Dordogne River to lay their eggs, and the leeks in the *marché* [market] are huge, it's time to *faire la lamproie*,' she says.

In her beautiful restored farmhouse with its stylish tiled kitchen, Dany enjoys cooking recipes handed down through the generations, much of the produce sourced from her own garden. This is the style of living that many of us aspire to – regional, seasonal, delicious.

REGIONAL FRANCE

During our travels we were lucky enough to have breakfast at Lyon's Les Halles Markets with the great Paul Bocuse. Paul is now a venerable old man of food, having spent over six decades in the kitchen working with the best produce, and it's no surprise that he believes France is the ultimate food and wine destination.

'France is the only country in the world to be a vineyard,' he told us. 'There's wine from north to south – in Burgundy, Beaujolais, Champagne, Bordeaux, the Loire Valley, Alsace and Costières de Nîmes. France is also a vegetable garden – vegetables are grown all over France. Plus we're the only country to be bathed by the North Sea, the Atlantic Ocean and the Mediterranean – of course that means wonderful seafood!'

There are twenty-two regions of France including the island of Corsica, and the food of each is prized.

Normandy on the north coast (comprising two official regions: Upper and Lower Normandy) produces some of the best butter, cream and cheese because of the rich pastures suited to dairying. There are also wonderful apples and seafood from the Atlantic.

West and south of Normandy are the regions of Brittany and Pays de la Loire, featuring a long sea coast and many bays that are the source of oysters, crayfish (spiny lobsters) and scallops, and the famous hand-harvested sea salt *sel de Guérande*. Buckwheat and crepes made of buckwheat flour are specialities of Brittany.

Champagne-Ardenne east of Paris is a great source of cheese such as maroilles, chaource and brie ... and of course it's the only place that produces sparkling wine that can legitimately be called Champagne!

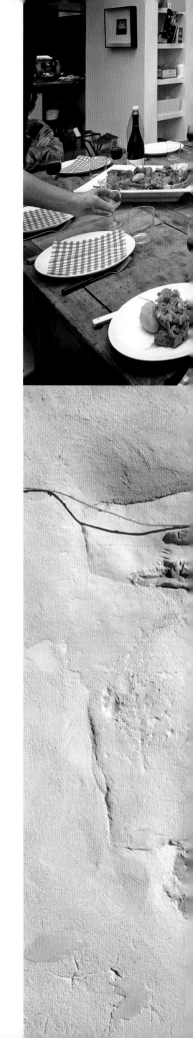

In the north-east towards Germany is Lorraine and Alsace, where you'll find quiche, *choucroute* – a hearty dish of sausage, pork, potatoes and sauerkraut – some wonderful white wines, rye bread and mountain berries.

Central France, which takes in the Loire Valley, is known for its vegetables, wild game and freshwater fish along with cherries, pears and strawberries, mushrooms and goat's cheese.

Burgundy and neighbouring Franche-Comté, which is next to Switzerland in the east, are of course known for burgundy wine and also charolais cattle, Bresse chicken, snails, freshwater fish, a range of cheese including comté, dijon mustard, nut oils and exquisite nougatine.

Rhône-Alpes bordering Switzerland and Italy includes the city of Lyon, which is considered the gastronomic capital and is well known for charcuterie. In the region you'll also find wine, walnuts and chestnuts, and alpine cheeses and cheese dishes such as fondue and raclette.

Provence-Alpes-Côte d'Azur in the south-east corner next to Italy produces heavenly lavender, herbs, olives and oil, truffles, honey, garlic, vegetables, citrus and other fruit, as well as seafood from the Mediterranean coast. It's also known for the anise-flavoured liqueur pastis, and specialist sweets such as *calissons* – leaf-shaped almond cakes flavoured with candied melon and orange, with royal icing.

Languedoc-Roussillon and Midi-Pyrénées in the south feature olives and olive oil, lamb, the dish cassoulet, and Roquefort cheese – the famous blue cheese matured in caves in Roquefort-sur-Soulzon.

Aquitaine in the south-west includes the area known as the Dordogne or Périgord, and also contains the Bordeaux wine region. Specialities are many and include duck and geese (and foie gras), truffles, nuts, prunes, sheep's cheese, *jambon de Bayonne* (air-dried salted ham), oysters from the coast, lamb – *agneau de Pauillac* – and espelette chilli, indicating that Spain is just over the border.

Auvergne in southern-central France is a mountainous region known for its cheese including cantal; charcuterie; and France's cherished puy lentils. To the west is Limousin and then Poitou-Charentes on the Atlantic coast. Together they boast cattle, oysters and mussels, mushrooms, goat's cheese and other first-class cheeses and butter.

Paris is located in the Île-de-France region, and to the north are the regions Picardy and then Nord Pas de Calais, which borders Belgium. Some of the specialities are eel, salt-marsh lamb and beer.

The Mediterranean island of Corsica is famous for goat, lamb and wild boar, seafood, chestnuts, citrus including clementines and citron, nectarines, figs and honey.

SOUP L'OIGNON

FRENCH ONION SOUP

from France Vidal

Serves 6

60 g (2 oz) unsalted butter

4–5 onions, finely sliced

50 g (1¾ oz/⅓ cup) plain (all-purpose) flour

2 litres (68 fl oz/8 cups) water

200 ml (7 fl oz) white wine

sea salt and freshly ground black pepper

100 g (3½ oz) gruyère, ½ cut into cubes and ½ grated

1 baguette

So simple, so perfect – this is a recipe that can make the world seem all right again. It originated as a hearty soup for Paris market workers who needed to warm themselves up on cold mornings. France Vidal loves it as her winter treat and prefers not to use stock as the basis, using water instead. She advises to buy the best brown onions – fresh with papery skins – and to cook them until deeply golden, as that's where all the depth of flavour and sweetness come from. She also says to use the best gruyère and baguette.

Melt the butter in a heavy-based saucepan and add the onion. Sauté for 25 minutes, stirring from time to time, until a deep golden brown.

Add the flour and stir for 2 minutes, then add the water and wine and season with salt and pepper. Stir in the cubes of cheese and bring to the boil, then reduce the heat, cover with a lid and simmer for 20–25 minutes. Check the seasoning.

Slice the baguette and sprinkle the slices with the grated cheese. Grill (broil) until the cheese melts.

Ladle the soup into bowls and serve with slices of grilled cheese baguette on top.

'THE PLEASURE OF THE TABLE BELONGS TO ALL AGES, TO ALL CONDITIONS, TO ALL COUNTRIES, AND TO ALL AREAS; IT MINGLES WITH ALL OTHER PLEASURES, AND REMAINS AT LAST TO CONSOLE US FOR THEIR DEPARTURE.'

Brillat-Savarin

CRIQUE ARDÈCHOIS

POTATO CAKE FROM THE ARDÈCHE

from Stéphane Reynaud in *365 good reasons to sit down and eat*

Serves 6

800 g (1 lb 12 oz) potatoes
(a floury variety such as coliban,
spunta or russet)

4 eggs, lightly beaten

3 small onions, finely chopped

1 bunch chives, finely chopped

sea salt and freshly ground
black pepper

olive oil

butter

This could be the best-ever potato cake, from our friend Stéphane Reynaud who was born and raised in the mountainous area of Ardèche in south-east France. The secret to the creamy texture is grating the potato very finely to produce a kind of raw potato purée. Stéphane likes to serve these potato cakes with a simple green salad of frisée (curly endive/chicory) with a mustard vinaigrette.

Peel the potatoes, then grate them on the finest side of a grater into a bowl (the potatoes should become a pulp). Mix in the eggs, then add the onion, chives, a generous pinch of salt and some pepper.

Add a splash of oil and a knob of butter to a frying pan and heat over medium heat until the butter is spitting. Add a large ladleful of potato mixture to the pan and reduce the heat to gentle. Cook the potato cake for 5–8 minutes, until golden brown, then flip and cook the other side. Remove to a plate and continue to cook more potato cakes with the rest of the mixture, adding extra oil and butter as needed.

'THE WORLD BELONGS TO THOSE WHO HAVE NO FIXED TIMES FOR MEALS.'
Anne Jules de Noailles, 17th century duke

Terroir and AOC

'Terroir' is the word you hear everywhere in France – it's the key to flavour; the reason everything from meat and vegetables to cheese and wine from different regions taste unique. The concept acknowledges that environmental factors such as soil and climate, and human factors such as farming methods, affect the characteristics and quality of products.

Hand in hand with terroir is France's system of *Appellation d'Origine Contrôlée*, which translates as 'controlled designation of origin'. This certification is granted to certain French wines, cheeses and other agricultural products, and decrees that the product is the best of the best – a great variety grown well in a great place.

The beginnings of the AOC system date back to the fifteenth century when Charles VI protected roquefort cheese by stating that only the cheese produced in Roquefort-sur-Soulzon and aged in the local caves could be sold under the name 'Roquefort'. The modern AOC system began in 1905 and now protects around three hundred wines and everything else from cheese and butter to fruit, vegetables, nuts, mustard, lentils, lavender, meat and poultry (see Bresse Chicken, page 14). AOC products are identified with a seal that is printed on their labels, and they are grown, raised or created to a strict set of standards that ensures they are the best they can be.

Bresse Chicken

Across France we saw so many signs of respect from farmers towards their produce, but nothing left such a lasting impression as the softly spoken poultry farmer Christian Picard. He's a second-generation farmer who just loves raising chickens on his pretty farm in Bresse, a former province in eastern France. He and his wife Véronique live in a picture-book thatched house overlooking rolling green fields, which are dotted with the white shapes of their flock out pecking for snails and insects. It's truly idyllic.

Christian took us to the old wooden shed where his chickens are fattened for market and knocked gently on the door. 'He likes to let the chickens know he's coming so they stay calm and happy,' whispered Véronique. These giants of chickens – some of them weighing around four kilograms (nine pounds) – seemed to respond to this gentle carer and allowed themselves to be picked up and shown off.

How different this is to poultry farms in many other parts of the world. Bresse chickens – the name of the breed as well as the place – are considered the very best, described by Brillat-Savarin in the nineteenth century as 'the queen of chickens and the chicken of kings'. The birds are distinct with their white feathers, red comb, and particularly their blue feet. The colours are a happy coincidence with the colours of the French flag.

All aspects of raising Bresse chickens are controlled by the *Appellation d'Origine Contrôlée* (AOC). The chicks stay in a warm, quiet barn for thirty-five days, roaming freely inside, and are then let out to green pastures where the law dictates that each chicken has ten square metres (108 square feet) of space dedicated to it. In the last few weeks of their lives, they are moved back to a warm barn to be fattened for market.

This tasty and most succulent chicken needs very little flavouring to cook it to perfection. Christian says he once tried supermarket chicken. 'I was forced to eat some,' he laughs. 'It's not at all the same – the texture's really awful!'

'Meat from a Bresse chicken is very firm under the knife,' he describes, 'but it melts in your mouth.'

BEEF BOURGUIGNON

from Guillaume Brahimi

Serves 6–8

125 ml (4 fl oz/½ cup) olive oil

1 kg (2 lb 3 oz) braising beef such as rump, topside or chuck steak (preferably wagyu), cut into large chunks

2 carrots, halved lengthways and sliced

2 celery stalks with leaves, halved lengthways and sliced

1 leek, white part only, halved lengthways and sliced

1 onion, chopped

5 French shallots, halved

500 ml (17 fl oz/2 cups) red wine

10 thyme sprigs

7 bay leaves

300 g (10½ oz) speck, diced

sea salt and freshly ground black pepper

300 g (10½ oz) button mushrooms

1 bunch flat-leaf (Italian) parsley, chopped

Carrot purée

5 carrots, chopped

This all-time favourite of slow-cooked beef with red wine and mushrooms will get you through winter. Speck adds a delicious smoky pork flavour and Guillaume's clever addition of carrot purée stirred through towards the end thickens the stew and adds extra colour and sweetness. Serve with Paris Mash (page 125) and fresh sourdough bread.

Heat the oil in a heavy-based pot over medium–high heat. Add the beef and cook until browned all over, then remove to a plate leaving most of the oil behind. Add the carrot, celery, leek, onion and shallots to the pot and sauté for 5–8 minutes.

While the vegetables are cooking, pour the wine into a small saucepan and bring to the boil. Simmer for a few minutes (this helps to reduce the acidity of the wine).

Return the beef to the pot of vegetables along with the thyme, bay leaves, speck, red wine and some salt and pepper. Stir to combine, then cover with a lid and simmer gently for 40 minutes.

Meanwhile, prepare the carrot purée by steaming or boiling the carrots until just soft. Drain and purée (or mash finely).

Add the carrot purée and whole mushrooms to the bourguignon and cook for a further 10 minutes.

Check the seasoning, stir in the parsley and serve.

COQ AU VIN

CHICKEN IN WINE

from Jacques Reymond

Serves 6

vegetable oil

2 medium onions, diced

2 carrots, diced

1 small beetroot (beet), diced

2 celery stalks, diced

½ garlic bulb, sliced in
half through the cloves

3 bay leaves

5 thyme sprigs

1 tablespoon black peppercorns

2 tablespoons sugar

2 × 750 ml (25½ fl oz) bottles
of pinot noir

1 × 1.6 kg (3½ lb) chicken

50 g (1¾ oz/⅓ cup) plain
(all-purpose) flour

sea salt and freshly ground
black pepper

2½ tablespoons red-wine
vinegar

100 ml (3½ fl oz) Veal Jus
(page 253)

roughly chopped flat-leaf (Italian)
parsley to serve

(ingredients continue page 21)

The original coq au vin – chicken braised in red wine – was made with
a rooster, which was often old and needed marinating and long cooking
to become tender and delicious. Today the stew is usually made with
chicken, and Melbourne chef Jacques Reymond comes from the part of
France where the world's best chickens are raised (see Bresse Chicken,
page 14). In fact, Jacques says his last meal on earth would be a Bresse
chicken because their texture and flavour is unsurpassed. In Australia,
you should source the best, plumpest free-range or organic chicken
you can find.

Jacques' version of coq au vin includes beetroot (beet) for extra
colour and sweetness, along with a separate sauce to serve on the side
that is thickened with chicken livers instead of the traditional blood.
Scattered on top of the stew is the 'grandmother garnish', a mixture of
sautéed shallots, kaiserfleisch or bacon, and button mushrooms. Coq au
vin is usually served with pasta such as pappardelle (ideally freshly made).

Heat a splash of oil in a large saucepan over medium heat and add the
diced vegetables and garlic pieces. Sauté until lightly coloured. Add the
bay leaves, thyme, peppercorns and sugar, then deglaze the pan with
1½ bottles of the wine. Bring to the boil. Remove from the heat and tip
into a large bowl to cool (to speed up the cooling, you can put the bowl
in the refrigerator).

Use a sharp knife to cut the chicken in half between the breasts and
through the spine. Cut each half into 3 large portions, giving 6 pieces
in total.

Once the wine and vegetable mixture is cold, add the chicken pieces
and weight down with a plate. Marinate in the refrigerator overnight.

'COOKING REQUIRES A LIGHT HEAD,
A GENEROUS SPIRIT AND A BIG HEART.'

Paul Gauguin, painter

Sauce

vegetable oil

½ onion, finely diced

1 small beetroot (beet),
finely diced

½ carrot, finely diced

½ celery stalk, finely diced

1 tablespoon sugar

250 ml (8½ fl oz/1 cup) pinot noir

250 g (9 oz) chicken livers, cleaned
and finely diced

Grandmother garnish

15 g (½ oz) clarified butter

6 French shallots, root ends
trimmed, peeled

1 tablespoon sugar

pinch of sea salt

100 ml (3½ fl oz) Chicken Stock
(page 250)

100 g (3½ oz) thick-cut kaiserfleisch
or bacon, sliced into batons

200 g (7 oz) small button
mushrooms

The next day, remove the chicken from the marinade and pat dry with paper towel. Lightly dust the chicken in the flour and season with salt and pepper.

Tip the marinade into a saucepan and bring to the boil. Meanwhile, heat a splash of oil in a heavy-based pot over medium heat and fry the chicken pieces until golden. Pour the hot marinade over the chicken and add the remaining wine along with the vinegar and jus. Cover with a lid and gently simmer for 35 minutes, or until the chicken is cooked through.

To make the sauce, heat a splash of oil in a medium saucepan and lightly sauté the vegetables. Add the sugar and cook for another minute, then add a third of the pinot noir. Allow to slightly reduce before adding the next third, and then the next. Ladle in half of the cooking liquid from the pot of chicken and simmer until reduced to a light sauce. Remove from the heat and whisk in the chicken livers for about 30 seconds to thicken the sauce. Strain the sauce immediately (if the livers are left in for too long, they will start to change the flavour of the sauce and can overpower it). Strain the sauce again and keep warm.

To make the grandmother garnish, heat half the butter in a small saucepan and add the shallots. Cook until their skins are nicely caramelised, then add the sugar and salt to caramelise further, cooking until the shallots are deeply glazed. Add the stock and simmer gently until the shallots are just soft and the liquid has almost evaporated.

Heat the remaining butter in a frying pan and fry the kaiserfleisch or bacon until golden. Add the mushrooms and sauté until golden, then add the shallots and heat through. Remove from the heat and drain off any excess butter.

Spread the grandmother garnish over the pot of warm chicken, and scatter with parsley. Serve on pasta drizzled with the extra sauce.

PISSALADIÈRE

from Philippe Mouchel in *Taste Le Tour*

Serves 8 as an appetiser

50 g (1¾ oz) butter

3 large onions, very finely sliced

sea salt and freshly ground black pepper

3 tablespoons extra-virgin olive oil

500 g (1 lb 2 oz) bread or pizza dough

around 20 anchovy fillets, drained

around 25 black olives

around 25 little thyme sprigs

France's answer to the pizza, pissaladière originated in Nice and can be made with a bread or pastry base, eaten hot or cold. It is full of the strong flavours of the south of France – onions, anchovies, thyme and olives, with no tomato required, as the sweetness of the onion alone is magic.

Heat the butter in a large frying pan. Add the onions and a little salt and pepper and cook over low heat for about 20 minutes, stirring from time to time, until lightly caramelised. It's important to cook the onions slowly as otherwise they can burn and taste unpleasant. Leave to cool slightly.

Preheat the oven to 190°C (375°F) and lightly brush a large square or rectangular tray with some of the oil.

Place the dough on the tray and use your hands to flatten it out to a rough square or rectangle about 5 mm (¼ in) thick. Brush the top of the dough with a little more oil.

Spread the cooked onion on top leaving a border of about 2 cm (¾ in) around the edges. Form the anchovies into lines about 5 cm (2 in) apart going diagonally across the onion. Make more lines of anchovies crisscrossing these lines, creating a diamond pattern. Place an olive and thyme sprig in each diamond. Season the pissaladière with pepper.

Bake in the oven for about 15 minutes, or until the base is golden and crisp. Brush the edges of the bread with a little more olive oil, then slice and serve. (Alternatively, let the pissaladière cool to room temperature before serving.)

CASSOULET

from Guillaume Brahimi

Serves 4

Duck confit

2 duck leg quarters

2 teaspoons sea salt

1 thyme sprig, leaves picked

1 bay leaf

1 garlic clove, bruised

400 ml (13½ fl oz) duck fat

1.5 litres (51 fl oz/6 cups) Veal Stock (page 253)

400 g (14 oz) pork neck, sliced into 4 steaks

1 small fresh pork hock

handful of thyme sprigs

1 garlic bulb

1 piece of pork skin (around 20 cm/8 in square), scored (optional)

90 g (3 oz) dried haricot or cannellini (lima) beans, soaked overnight

200 g (7 oz) piece of pork belly

½ teaspoon sea salt

3 toulouse sausages (or other quality pork sausages)

1 small carrot, finely chopped

1 small onion, finely chopped

1 small tomato, finely chopped

1 loaf of brioche

This glorious celebration of rustic French cooking comes from Languedoc in the south of France. A mix of haricot beans, different cuts of pork, sausages and duck confit baked with a crispy bread topping, cassoulet is traditionally made in a tall earthenware pot that is narrow at the base and wide at the top to give the maximum amount of crust. Guillaume's recipe includes making your own duck confit, which you should start the day before (along with soaking the beans). Cassoulet is perfect served alongside Leaf and Chive Salad with Shallot Vinaigrette (page 62) to add some bite to the rich and hearty dish.

The day before serving, prepare the duck confit by putting the duck leg quarters in a bowl and rubbing them with the salt, thyme, bay leaf and garlic. Refrigerate overnight.

The next day, preheat the oven to 150°C (300°F). Rinse the duck, pat it dry, and place in a small, deep roasting pan. Bring the duck fat to the boil in a saucepan, then pour over the leg quarters to cover. (Alternatively, if you have an ovenproof saucepan, you could simply submerge the leg quarters in the saucepan of hot fat.) Bake the duck in the oven for 1½–2 hours, or until soft. Remove from the oven and leave to cool in the fat.

Bring the stock to a simmer in an ovenproof pot. While it is heating, place a frying pan over medium–high heat and add a generous scoop of fat from the duck. Put the pork-neck steaks into the pan and fry until golden brown on each side. Remove to a plate and brown the pork hock all over.

Add the steaks and hock to the simmering stock along with the thyme and whole garlic bulb. Place the pork skin over the top of the meat like a lid to keep the pork moist and ensure the stock doesn't reduce too quickly (alternatively, you can use a piece of baking paper). Simmer the pork for 1 hour.

Meanwhile, drain the beans and place in a saucepan with fresh water. Bring to the boil, then drain immediately and refresh under cold water.

Add the blanched beans to the pot of pork and stock and simmer for a further hour.

(As an alternative to cooking the pork and beans on the stovetop, they can be braised in the oven).

Rub the pork belly with the salt and leave to rest for 20 minutes. Reheat the oven to 200°C (400°F) and place the pork on a tray skin-side up. Roast until the skin is crispy, then remove from the oven and leave to rest.

Reheat the frying pan used to fry the pork (there should still be some fat in the pan) and add the sausages, frying until golden. Add the carrot, onion and tomato and sauté for 5 minutes. Add a splash of stock from the pot of pork and beans and cook until the carrots are soft. Set aside.

Heat a separate frying pan over high heat. Remove the duck from its fat and cut each leg quarter in half. Place in the pan skin-side down and sear until crisp on each side.

Remove the pork skin from the pot of pork and beans and discard. Take out the pork neck, hock and garlic bulb from the pot, and remove the sausages from the frying pan. Take the meat off the hock bone and chop into generous pieces. Slice the pork neck and sausages into chunks. Slice the roasted pork belly into 4 pieces. Return all the sliced meat and the fried duck confit to the pot of beans.

Place the garlic on the chopping board and separate into cloves. Use the side of a knife to squeeze the pulp from each clove, then finely chop the pulp.

Add the garlic purée and vegetables from the frying pan to the pot of meat and beans and stir gently to combine.

Reheat the oven to 200°C (400°F). Cut the crusts from the loaf of brioche and discard. Slice the remaining brioche and toast the slices in the oven until golden. Stack the slices on top of each other and dice. Crumble into smaller pieces over the surface of the cassoulet. Bake the cassoulet in the oven for 10 minutes, or until hot through and the crumbs are golden.

SOUFFLÉ AU FROMAGE

CHEESE SOUFFLÉ

from Marie-Helene Clauzon

A mix of simple ingredients and clever techniques makes the light and creamy masterpiece that is soufflé. Use the best cheese you can source and serve straight away!

Serves 4–6

60 g (2 oz) butter

60 g (2 oz) plain (all-purpose) flour

500 ml (17 fl oz/2 cups) milk

200 g (7 oz) gruyère, grated

sea salt and freshly ground black pepper

freshly grated nutmeg

6 eggs, separated

Preheat the oven to 200°C (400°F) and butter a large soufflé dish.

To make a roux, melt the butter in a heavy-based saucepan over low heat. Add the flour, stirring with a wooden spoon until the mixture forms a thick paste. Swap the spoon for a whisk and add the milk in small amounts, whisking it into the flour. Cook the mixture until smooth and thick, then remove from the heat.

Whisk in the cheese and season to taste with salt, pepper and nutmeg. Whisk in the egg yolks.

In a large bowl, beat the egg whites with a pinch of salt to stiff peaks – they should be firm but not dry. Stir a little egg white into the saucepan of cheese mixture to loosen it. Then pour the cheese mixture into the bowl of egg whites and fold together gently.

Pour the mixture into the soufflé dish and smooth the top. Bake in the centre of the oven for 10 minutes. Turn the oven down to 180°C (350°F) and cook for another 25–30 minutes, until risen and golden brown. Serve immediately.

'A GOOD COOK IS LIKE A SORCERESS WHO DISPENSES HAPPINESS.'
Elsa Schiaparelli, 20th century Paris fashion designer

Cheese Plate

Serving a cheese course French-style needs a little planning. Like the rules underpinning French fashion, you need to buy well and carefully – quality over quantity every time. Australia's guru of cheese, Will Studd, says to remember that the best impact can sometimes be made with just a single cheese.

'It's very important to remember that one great cheese in perfect condition is much better than five or six cheeses in just average condition. So one of my personal delights is to sit and enjoy a piece of Roquefort that's seasonally perfect, with some rye bread and some sauternes in a nice place. You can't beat that!' says Will, who has studied cheese for over thirty years and been recognised as a Master of Cheese by the French *Guilde des Fromagers*.

Cheese 'in perfect condition' is cheese that has been cared for and brought to maturity by what is called an *affineur* in France. Attached to the top cheese shops, this profession is held in high regard – *affineurs* are craftsmen in their own right, selecting the best cheeses and ageing them carefully, deciding when they're at their best to release to the public. Some cheeses are turned daily to ensure they ripen evenly, while others need washing or brushing to assist fermentation and develop creaminess. The work of an *affineur* refines the cheese maker's product to something truly exceptional.

Here are some more tips from Will on serving cheese:

Great cheese will only reveal its true flavour and texture when served at the right temperature, which is generally room temperature, although adjustments need to be made in very hot or cold weather. In hot weather take the cheese out of the refrigerator 1 hour before serving; in cold weather take it out up to 4 hours before serving, but leave it in its waxed paper or cover with a damp cloth so it won't dry out.

Serve cheese on a natural material like wood, marble, ceramic or seasonal leaves – never on plastic or metal.

Leave space on the plate between each cheese you are serving, and serve each with a separate knife.

'A DESSERT WITHOUT CHEESE IS LIKE A
BEAUTIFUL WOMAN WITH ONLY ONE EYE.'
Brillat-Savarin

The worst sin you can commit is to cut the 'nose' off a wedge of cheese – good manners dictate it should be cut from the side.

Taste cheeses from the mildest through to the strongest, finishing with blue cheese.

Bread is the perfect accompaniment – it's another natural product and it helps to balance the flavours of the cheese and enhance its sensual texture. Aim to serve quality artisanal bread.

Fresh cheeses and soft cheeses ripened with surface mould such as brie and camembert are best served with bread that is not too strong in flavour, for instance baguettes or light sourdough. **Soft washed-rind cheeses** like munster and vacherin with their aromatic and yeasty flavours are great with fruit breads or rye. **Blue cheeses** like Roquefort are perfect with sourdough, pumpernickel or walnut bread. Semi-hard pressed cheeses like cantal with their tangy flavours go with a whole range of breads. **Hard pressed cheeses** like beaufort – dense, nutty and perfumed – are magic on their own, although Will suggests gruyère should be served with walnut or fruit bread.

POT-AU-FEU

BEEF STEW

from Guillaume Brahimi

Serves 4–6

water

1.5 kg (3 lb 5 oz) beef short ribs
(or 800 g/1 lb 12 oz braising beef,
cut into large chunks)

1 tablespoon sea salt

freshly ground black pepper

bouquet garni of bay leaves
and sprigs of parsley and thyme
(tied together with string)

2 onions, peeled and studded
with cloves

2 leeks, white part only,
thickly sliced

2 celery stalks, cut into large
chunks

6 medium potatoes, peeled and
cut into large chunks

3 large carrots, peeled and cut
into large chunks

2 turnips, peeled and quartered

This hearty stew has been referred to as 'the foundation of empires', an ancient dish prepared in a deep pot traditionally made with a variety of cuts of meat along with vegetables and herbs, all simply cooked in water. It's even better the day after it's made, as the fat can be skimmed off the surface and the flavours really develop. This dish was a showstopper when chef and author Stéphane Reynaud made it for us on the cold November day when we visited his home in Saint-Agrève. Here is Guillaume's version of the dish. The broth of the stew is traditionally served on the side, but if desired it can be served together with the meat and vegetables. Serve dijon mustard (for stirring in to taste) and cornichons on the side.

Half-fill a pot with water. Add the meat, salt and some pepper and bring to a simmer, skimming the surface of any foam and impurities. Add the bouquet garni, onions, leek and celery and cook gently, uncovered, for 2 hours, skimming the surface whenever necessary and adding more water if it gets very low.

Add the potato, carrot and turnip and simmer for another 35 minutes, or until the vegetables are tender.

Scoop the meat and vegetables from the broth into a dish. Strain the broth through a piece of muslin (cheesecloth) and serve with the meat and vegetables.

'LE MOUTARDE ME MONTÉ AU NEZ.'

(To lose your temper; let the mustard get up your nose.)

BRIOCHE

from Guillaume Brahimi

Makes 2 large or 16 small brioche

100 ml (3½ fl oz) milk

20 g (¾ oz) (or 3 × 7 g/¼ oz sachets) dried yeast

500 g (1 lb 2 oz/3⅓ cups) plain (all-purpose) flour

2 teaspoons salt

50 g (1¾ oz/¼ cup) caster (superfine) sugar

5 eggs, plus 1 for the egg wash

300 g (10½ oz) unsalted butter at room temperature, diced

This sweet yeast bread enriched with butter and eggs is adored throughout France. It is easy enough to make at home, smells divine as it cooks and, while you would either need to get up early or make it the day before, it forms the perfect centrepiece of a weekend breakfast. Enjoy with jam or dunked into coffee or hot chocolate.

Heat the milk in a small saucepan to lukewarm. Pour into a small bowl and add the yeast, stirring to dissolve.

Put the flour, salt, sugar and eggs into an electric mixer fitted with a dough hook. Mix at low speed until just combined, then gradually add the milk and yeast mixture. Stop the mixer from time to time to scrape down the side of the bowl. Once the mixture is well combined, increase the speed to medium and knead for about 10 minutes – by the end the dough should be smooth and elastic.

With the mixer running on low speed, start adding the butter a few pieces at a time. Once you have added all the butter, turn the speed up to high and knead the dough for a further 6–10 minutes, until smooth, shiny and pulling away easily from the sides of the bowl. Cover with a tea towel (dish towel) and leave to rise in a warm place until doubled in size (this takes around 2 hours when the temperature is at 24°C/75°F).

Butter 2 large fluted brioche tins (or 16 small tins). Turn the dough out onto a lightly floured work surface, knocking the air out of the dough. If making 2 large brioche, divide the dough into a large piece (about two-thirds of the dough) and a smaller piece (about one-third). Divide both pieces in half and shape each piece into a ball. Place the large balls in the bottom of the tins. Use your finger to make a dent in the middle and sit the small balls in the dents.

If making small brioche, divide the dough into 16 pieces. Then, divide each piece into a large piece and small piece, shape into balls and follow the same instructions. Cover the tins with a tea towel and leave to rise in a warm place until the brioche has doubled in size (around 1½ hours).

Preheat the oven to 180°C (350°F). Beat the egg for the egg wash and lightly brush it over the brioche. Bake large brioche for 35–40 minutes and small brioche for 20 minutes, or until golden and hollow-sounding when tapped. Leave to cool in the tins for 5 minutes before turning out onto a rack to cool.

LAMB NAVARIN

from Philippe Mouchel

Serves 8–10

100 ml (3½ fl oz) vegetable oil

150 g (5½ oz) unsalted butter

1 kg (2 lb 3 oz) boned lamb shoulder, cut into 5 cm (2 in) cubes

1 kg (2 lb 3 oz) forequarter lamb racks, cut between every second rib

200 g (7 oz) onions, diced

200 g (7 oz) carrots, diced

1 tablespoon plain (all-purpose) flour

250 ml (8½ fl oz/1 cup) dry white wine

4 tomatoes, diced

1 turnip, peeled and diced

1 rosemary sprig

1 thyme sprig

1 bay leaf

4 garlic cloves, roughly chopped

Chicken Stock (page 250) or water

sea salt and freshly ground black pepper

250 g (9 oz) baby onions or French shallots, trimmed and peeled

1 teaspoon sugar

1 kg (2 lb 3 oz) kipfler (fingerling) potatoes

300 g (10½ oz) baby carrots with some green stem remaining if desired, peeled

300 g (10½ oz) baby turnips with some green stem remaining if desired, peeled

80 g (2¾ oz/½ cup) peas

Celeriac purée

1 kg (2 lb 3 oz) celeriac, peeled and cut into chunks

500 ml (17 fl oz/2 cups) milk

sea salt

200 g (7 oz) unsalted butter, diced

freshly ground black pepper

grated truffle (optional)

A beautiful winter stew from Normandy combining lamb, turnips (*navets*), carrots and potatoes. Philippe uses lamb shoulder and ribs cut into large pieces, but the dish also works well with lamb necks. He likes to serve it with celeriac purée and believes cooking the celeriac in milk helps to retain its lovely pale colour.

Heat the oil with a large knob of the butter in a heavy-based pot. Add the lamb pieces and cook until browned all over. Remove the lamb to a plate.

Add the diced onion and carrot and a little more butter to the pot and cook for another 5 minutes, stirring well. Drain off the excess fat if there now seems to be too much, then stir in the flour and cook for another minute or so. Return the lamb to the pot and pour in the wine. Simmer until slightly reduced, then add the tomato, diced turnip, rosemary, thyme, bay leaf and garlic, and enough chicken stock or water to come up to the level of the lamb. Season with salt and pepper, cover with a lid and simmer for 1 hour.

Meanwhile, heat the remaining butter in a small saucepan and add the baby onions or shallots, the sugar and some salt. Cook, stirring, until lightly browned, then add a little chicken stock or water and bring to the boil. Cook over low heat until soft.

Bring a large saucepan of water to the boil and add the potatoes. Boil for 5 minutes, then drain.

Ladle the lamb from the pot, then strain the sauce through a fine sieve. Return the sauce to the pot along with the pieces of lamb and the whole potatoes. Cover and simmer for another 15 minutes.

To make the celeriac purée, put the celeriac in a saucepan with the milk, some salt and enough water to just cover. Boil until soft, then drain. Return to the pan and mash, adding the butter piece by piece. Season with salt and pepper to taste and stir through some grated truffle if desired. Keep warm.

After the potatoes have been simmering with the lamb for 15 minutes, add the baby onions or shallots, and the baby carrots and turnips and continue to simmer until tender. Add the peas for the last 10 minutes.

Serve the lamb, vegetables and sauce with the celeriac purée.

MARKETS

MARKETS

For a food lover, there is no experience more sensual than strolling through a French produce market. It's a total feast, from the beautiful colours of the vegetables and fruit so carefully displayed, to the fresh bunches of herbs, the wheels of cheese at ripe perfection, and the sounds of business being conducted all around. This is the antidote to the sterile supermarket full of vacuum-packed goods on styrofoam trays. Sometimes the farmers serve you themselves, and if not, the providore has a high grade of knowledge and is happy to pass it on, so that you really know what you are buying and how to cook or serve it.

One rule of etiquette is you never touch the produce yourself – one must be served by the stallholder. They ask you when you intend to eat what you're purchasing and pick accordingly, and the French people trust their stallholder wholeheartedly.

Every neighbourhood in France's big cities has a market once or twice a week, as do the towns and villages. They are an integral part of French life and the thing expatriates miss the most – the time-honoured ritual of strolling the market and seeing what produce is in season so you can put meaningful thought into your next meal. Even the small street markets have an amazing selection of produce – fruit and vegetables, cheese, pastries and bread, charcuterie, fish, separate stalls for poultry, beef, pork, and offal (variety meats/the *triperies*), and flowers and spices.

As part of our odyssey through France filming *French Food Safari*, we were lucky enough to spend some pre-dawn hours at the Rungis International Market, the world's biggest wholesale produce market on the outskirts of Paris. In a series of enormous halls spread over an area the size of a suburb, the market hums with forklifts whizzing around crates of the world's finest produce – pheasants from Scotland, sea urchins from Iceland (destined for plates by lunchtime), oranges from Israel, bananas from South America, and of course food from all over France. Visiting Rungis is like walking through a living food encyclopedia, and while it is closed to the general public, you can visit as part of a tour.

The workers wear identical white coats, giving the market the feel of an enormous science lab, and many affect a distinctive hat or scarf or, for some of the men, a handlebar moustache. The beef section is surreal with a vast sea of carcasses hanging from hooks. In another area hang the legs.

Rungis's turnover is a staggering seven billion dollars (4.5 billion pounds) a year. As well as containing all the produce you could dream of, it has some wonderful workers' cafes where the coffee is good and strong – just what you need in the small hours of the morning. The baguettes filled with wedges of brie are legendary.

As food tourism grows, more and more travellers seek out markets as a key to the essence of a place, and the city of Lyon has another market worth crossing the world for. The Les Halles Market is a little friendlier than Rungis – there's no harsh lighting and each stall seems to have a warm golden glow. The shop owners dress in perfect starched uniforms and have the sort of professional attitude in looking after their customers that could set an example for anyone training in hospitality.

The cafes and little restaurants within Les Halles are full of all ages of customers enjoying food and wine in between shopping. We noticed a group of young people who looked like they had been out dancing all night and had stopped in for some crusty bread and slices of *jambon* (ham) and *saucisson* (salami) on their way home. How marvellous that they weren't guzzling fast food but opting for charcuterie, which is something Lyon prides itself on.

Among the many stallholders in Lyon, you notice one or two who are obviously bosses wearing a chef's jacket with the tricolour – red, white and blue – at the collar. They are the kings of their craft wearing the mark of the *Meilleur Ouvrier de France*, a unique award celebrating the best food craftsmen in respective areas. Every four years a competition is held for butchers, pâtissiers, chocolatiers and others. These craftsmen show off their technical skills, innovation and respect for produce and tradition, and are judged by their peers and later awarded medals by the president. The awards are for life and the winners become ambassadors of their trade, sharing their knowledge and training people for the future.

In the spirit of the fresh and abundant produce market, this chapter features some of France's great vegetable dishes, from the elegant combination of asparagus with hollandaise, to the celebration of summer that is Provence's ratatouille. Scattered through the book you will also find many miraculous ways that the French cook the humble potato – proof that some of the best French cooking is a mix of simple ingredients and clever techniques.

'LÂCHE PAS LA PATATE.'
(Don't give up; don't drop the potato.)

RATATOUILLE

from Guillaume Brahimi

Serves 6

extra-virgin olive oil

2 eggplants (aubergines), diced

3 garlic cloves, finely chopped

sea salt and freshly
ground black pepper

4 zucchini (courgettes), diced

½ bunch thyme, leaves
picked

1 onion, diced

2 red capsicums (bell peppers),
diced

1 kg (2 lb 3 oz) tomatoes, seeded
and diced

500 ml (17 fl oz/2 cups)
tomato juice

1 bunch basil, chopped

From Provence in the south of France, this simple dish sings with summer vegetables – eggplant (aubergine), zucchini (courgette), capsicum (bell pepper) and tomato. Guillaume likes to cook the vegetables separately first, then combine them to cook to a glorious creamy stew that reminds him of childhood summers spent in Provence. Ratatouille was made before the family went to the beach and the flavours were perfectly melded by the time they arrived home.

Heat a generous splash of oil in a frying pan over low heat and add the eggplant and a third of the garlic. Season with salt and pepper and sauté until tender. Tip into a large bowl.

Return the pan to the heat and add more oil. Add the zucchini, another third of the garlic, half the thyme and some salt and pepper. Sauté until tender, then add to the bowl with the eggplant.

Add more oil to the pan and sauté the onion, capsicum and remaining garlic and thyme until tender.

Combine all the cooked vegetables in a pot. Add the tomatoes and juice and simmer gently for 1½ hours. Remove from the heat, taste for seasoning and stir in the basil.

'THE BEST COOKING IS THAT WHICH TAKES INTO CONSIDERATION THE PRODUCTS OF THE SEASON.'
Fernand Point, 20th century chef and restaurateur

GRATIN DAUPHINOIS

POTATO GRATIN

from Guillaume Brahimi

Serves 4–6

500 ml (17 fl oz/2 cups) milk

250 ml (8½ fl oz/1 cup) pouring (single/light) cream

1 garlic clove, half finely sliced, half left whole

1 kg (2 lb 3 oz) desiree or other all-purpose potatoes, peeled and finely sliced

pinch of freshly grated nutmeg

140 g (5 oz) gruyère, grated

sea salt and freshly ground white pepper

chopped flat-leaf (Italian) parsley

This is the ultimate indulgence for potato lovers – layered potatoes baked in cream and butter from the Dauphiné, a former province of south-east France. Forget the diet for a moment and enjoy this with any grilled meats or roasts.

Bring the milk and cream to the boil in a large saucepan over medium heat. Remove from the heat and stir in the sliced garlic, followed by the potatoes, nutmeg and a handful of the grated cheese. Stir well, then return to the heat and simmer until the potatoes have started to soften.

Preheat the oven to 200°C (400°F). Rub the inside of a large baking dish with butter, then rub with the remaining half clove of garlic. Season the potato mixture to taste and spoon a layer into the dish. Sprinkle with some cheese and add more potatoes. Continue to layer until you have used up the potatoes, finishing with a layer of cheese. Bake in the oven for 20–30 minutes, or until golden brown and crisp on top. Sprinkle with parsley to serve.

'SE REFILER LA PATATE CHAUDE.'

(To pass on the troublesome matter; pass the hot potato.)

POTAGE SAINT-GERMAIN
PEA AND LETTUCE SOUP
from Guillaume Brahimi

Serves 4

15 g (½ oz) unsalted butter

1 leek, white part only, finely chopped

750 ml (25½ fl oz/3 cups) Chicken Stock (page 250)

465 g (1 lb/3 cups) peas (fresh or frozen)

2 cups chopped lettuce

sea salt and freshly ground black pepper

This simple and fresh-tasting soup is said to be named after the intriguing Count of Saint-Germain, who was employed in diplomatic services in eighteenth-century France and was renowned for his ever-youthful appearance. The soup is traditionally made in spring when peas and lettuce are abundant in the garden, but frozen peas now make it a dish we can enjoy any day.

Heat the butter to foaming in a large saucepan. Add the leek and sauté until soft. Pour in the chicken stock and bring to the boil, then add the peas and lettuce and simmer for 10 minutes, or until the peas are tender. Purée the soup and season to taste. Serve with croutons and a swirl of crème fraîche.

'OF ALL THE ITEMS ON THE MENU, SOUP IS THAT WHICH EXACTS THE MOST DELICATE PERFECTION AND THE STRICTEST ATTENTION.'
Auguste Escoffier

POMMES FRITES

FRENCH FRIES

from Guillaume Brahimi

desiree or other all-purpose potatoes (allow 2 potatoes per person)

vegetable oil

sea salt

If there's one French invention that has conquered the world, it has to be thin, straw-like batons of fried potato – French fries. American president Thomas Jefferson recorded these delicious potatoes being served to him by his French chef in the early nineteenth century, and this is said to be the first appearance of French fries in America.

The secret to perfect *frites* is to cook them twice. Some devotees also swear that frying them in duck fat makes them even more delicious as the fat is especially flavoursome, and it can be heated to a higher temperature than oil to crisp and brown the fries quickly.

Peel the potatoes, then cut off their rounded ends and sides to form blocks. Cut the blocks into slices about 5 mm (¼ in) thick. Stack the slices on top of each other and cut into 5 mm (¼ in) wide batons.

Immerse the potatoes in a bowl of cold water, swirling them around to remove the starch. Tip out the water and refill with more cold water, swirling again. Drain the potatoes, then wrap in a tea towel (dish towel) and shake dry as you would salad leaves. Place the potatoes on a dry tea towel to air until frying.

Pour oil into a large heavy-based saucepan to around two-thirds full, making sure there will be no less than twice as much oil to potatoes (the potatoes can be cooked in batches if making a large quantity). Heat the oil to 140°C (285°F) and add the potatoes. Allow the potatoes to fry gently for about 5 minutes, until soft and pale. Scoop from the oil and drain on paper towel. You can keep these part-cooked potatoes at room temperature for up to 3 hours.

When ready to serve, reheat the oil to 180°C (350°F) and return the potatoes to the pan. Fry vigorously for 2–3 minutes, until golden and crisp. Remove from the oil and drain briefly on paper towel. Season with salt and serve immediately.

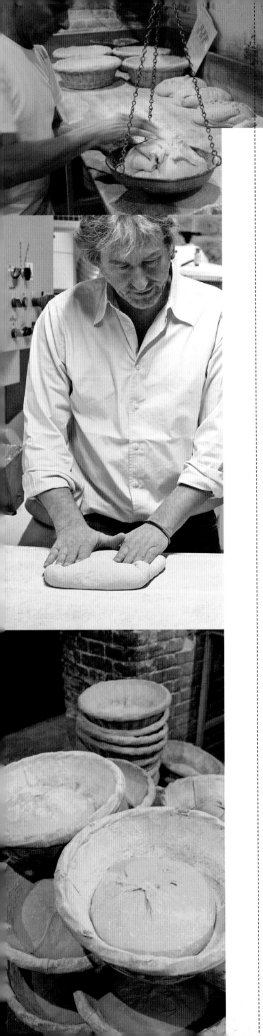

Bread

In France people's lives are punctuated by their visits to the *boulangerie* – the bakery. Children grow up with the responsibility of buying the family's bread, while for some elderly people their visit to the bakery is a social event that brightens their day. Enlightened bakeries like the well-known Poilâne in Paris sell bread by the piece or slice.

Underneath Poilâne's warm little shop in Saint-Germain, down the narrow stairs, is a wood-fired oven that hasn't cooled down since it was first lit in the 1930s. The bread made here really is exceptional – the signature sourdough is an old-fashioned country loaf weighing almost two kilograms (four and a half pounds), with a nice thick crust. It stays delicious for a whole week. Some locals actually refer to 'buying a Poilâne' rather than buying a loaf of bread, and the bread is even flown daily into New York and Tokyo to adoring fans.

This type of bread was the mainstay in France before the thin white loaf with a crisp golden crust – the baguette, a symbol of France – became popular in the nineteenth century.

Across town and also underground is the bakery of bread rock-star Jean-Luc Poujauran, whose bread is on many of the best tables in Paris. Jean-Luc doesn't sell to the public, but his exacting methods and the flavour of his loaves have rocketed him into the stratosphere of great bakers. His sourdough starter is over seventy years old, passed onto him from his father.

Bread is 'a cultural thing', says Jean-Luc. 'In France, from a very early age, they give you a coin and say, "Go and get the bread." In the country it's a child's daily task.' The French people build up a relationship with their bakers, Jean-Luc explains. 'A baker works at night. Like the doctor, he's someone we trust. We get our morning bread, fresh and warm. A good baker is a wonderful man. I speak on behalf of all bakers.'

Jean-Luc's fragrant loaves are made with stone-ground flour, *sel de Guérande* (sea salt from the west coast of France) and water, with the starter breathing life into the beautiful ingredients. The bread takes three days to make and prove, and when Guillaume Brahimi took a deep sniff of a freshly baked loaf, he closed his eyes and breathed, 'Now that's bread!'.

'LONG COMME UN JOUR SANS PAIN.'
(As long as a day without bread.)

Here are some of France's classic breads:

Baguette: A long, thin, white loaf with a golden crust. It is raised with commercial yeast and has an open crumb and large holes. This light style of bread is best eaten the day it is bought.

Ficelle: Using the same ingredients and methods as the baguette, but even thinner and sometimes shorter.

Pain de campagne: Translating as 'country bread', this is a large round or rectangular bread usually made with a mixture of white flour and wholemeal (whole-wheat) or rye flour. It can be made with natural leavening or commercial yeast.

Pain au levain: Made with natural leavening, this is rustic and flavoursome sourdough.

Fougasse: Typically associated with Provence, this flatbread is France's version of the focaccia. The dough is often slashed so it looks like an ear of wheat, and is usually dotted with ingredients such as olives or cheese.

Pain aux noix: Studded with one of France's favourite ingredients – walnuts – this bread is delicious with cheese.

TOMATO SALAD

from Guillaume Brahimi

Serves 4

750 g (1 lb 11 oz) mixed
small heirloom tomatoes

½ bunch flat-leaf (Italian) parsley,
finely sliced

60 ml (2 fl oz/¼ cup) extra-virgin
olive oil

1 tablespoon balsamic
vinegar

sea salt and freshly ground
black pepper

Use only the ripest and most flavoursome summer tomatoes for this
salad. Heirloom tomatoes of many varieties and colours are in vogue,
but Guillaume says that any full-flavoured tomato will work well. Then
all you need to do is to invest in a good oil and vinegar.

Slice the larger tomatoes in half and leave the smaller ones whole.
Put them in a bowl and scatter with the parsley. Dress with the oil
and vinegar, season to taste, and toss to combine.

'AVOIR DE LA BOUTEILLE.'
(To gain wisdom with age like a good bottle of wine.)

AUTUMN AND WINTER VEGETABLES AND FRUITS *EN COCOTTE*

from Alain Ducasse in *Nature*

Serves 4

1 apple

1 pear

juice of 1 lemon

4 salsify if available,
or 1 parsnip

3 tablespoons olive oil

2 thick slices of bacon

4 baby carrots with some
green stem remaining, peeled
and cut into large chunks

4 baby turnips with some
green stem remaining, peeled
and quartered

4 celery stalks, cut into large
chunks

1 red (Spanish) onion, cut into
large chunks

1 quince, peeled, cored and
cut into 1.5 cm (¾ in) cubes

handful of peeled chestnuts
(can be frozen or vacuum-
packed)

sea salt

200 ml (7 fl oz) Chicken Stock
(page 250)

16 green grapes

sherry vinegar

This is a domestic version of a famous dish served at Ducasse's Paris restaurant at the Plaza Athénée. It's a complex yet simple recipe that underlines the supreme chef's desire to put vegetables and sustainable agriculture under the spotlight. The vegetables and fruits with their range of gold and russet tones are cooked in their own jus with the addition of a little stock, in a heavy pot known in French as a *cocotte*. The vegetables must be cooked until just soft enough; the apples and pears hardly at all. You'll find the vinegar adds a mellow touch of acidity. This elegant dish is perfect served with any roast meat.

Peel, quarter and core the apple and pear and place in a bowl of cold water with the lemon juice added to stop them from discolouring.

If using salsify, peel them and finely slice on an angle. If using parsnip, peel and cut as per the carrots.

Heat the oil in a pot and fry the bacon slices until browned on each side. Remove to a plate. Add the apple and pear to the pot and allow the pieces to colour on all sides, then remove to the plate. Add the salsify or parsnip, carrot, turnip, celery, onion, quince and chestnuts to the pot. Season with salt and cook, stirring occasionally, for around 3 minutes to lightly brown the ingredients. Pour in the chicken stock, cover with a lid and simmer over low heat for 10–12 minutes, or until the ingredients are tender when tested with the tip of a knife.

Meanwhile, cut the browned bacon into thin strips (lardons).

Add the apple, pear, grapes and bacon to the pot. Stir very gently and add a splash of sherry vinegar. Stir again and serve straight from the pot.

'EACH GOOD PRODUCT, GROWN WITH LOVE AND RESPECT,
IN ITS DISTINCTIVE LAND, HAS AN INCOMPARABLE FLAVOUR.
WITHOUT WHICH, A CHEF IS NOTHING.'

Alain Ducasse

LEAF AND CHIVE SALAD WITH SHALLOT VINAIGRETTE

from Guillaume Brahimi

Serves 4

Vinaigrette

3 large French shallots, finely sliced

2 tablespoons good-quality red-wine vinegar

80 ml (2½ fl oz/⅓ cup) extra-virgin olive oil

sea salt and freshly ground white pepper

300 g (10½ oz) mixed young salad leaves such as radicchio, frisée (curly endive/chicory), butter (Boston) lettuce, cos (romaine) and witlof (Belgian endive/chicory), washed and dried

2 tablespoons finely chopped chives

Salads are an important part of the French meal, adding freshness and crispness to meat dishes, stews, soufflés and just about anything. (In fact, they are traditionally eaten as a cleansing course after the main meal.) A good green salad is simply made with fresh leaves that have been thoroughly washed and dried (investing in a salad spinner is worthwhile), then tossed gently by hand with a nicely balanced and seasoned vinaigrette. Guillaume's shallot vinaigrette gives the basic green salad a little extra bite, so it's perfect with rich or hearty dishes such as Cassoulet (page 24).

Put the shallots and vinegar in a blender and blitz until combined without letting the shallots become too finely chopped. Pour in the oil as you continue to blend, then quickly turn off the motor. Pour into a jar and season to taste with salt and pepper. This quantity makes enough for approximately 2 salads and can be stored in the refrigerator for up to 1 week.

To make the salad, combine the leaves, chives and about half the vinaigrette in a bowl and toss gently with your hands. Taste and add more vinaigrette if desired.

WHY ARE THE FRENCH SO GOOD AT MAKING CHEESE? 'IT'S BECAUSE WE HAVE TASTE BUDS!'

Jérôme Herphelin, cheese maker

SALADE D'HIVER

WINTER SALAD

from Guillaume Brahimi

Serves 4

50 g (1¾ oz) sultanas (golden raisins)

6 witlof (Belgian endive/chicory)

80 ml (2½ fl oz/⅓ cup) olive oil

2 tablespoons canola oil

2 tablespoons white-wine vinegar

sea salt and freshly ground black pepper

150 g (5½ oz) Roquefort cheese

50 g (1¾ oz) fresh walnuts

Winter salads vary across the regions of France, usually using bitter salad leaves like witlof (Belgian endive/chicory) or frisée (curly endive/chicory), or watercress, with additions of celery, nuts, dried or fresh fruit, and sometimes cheese to add creaminess. They make great accompaniments to rich dishes like duck confit or roast pork.

Soak the sultanas in warm water for 15 minutes, then drain.

Cut the witlof into quarters and remove the cores. Separate the leaves and place in a salad bowl.

Whisk the oils and vinegar together and season with salt and pepper.

Crumble the Roquefort on top of the witlof. Add the walnuts and sultanas, then pour over the dressing. Toss well and serve.

ASPARAGUS WITH HOLLANDAISE SAUCE

from Guillaume Brahimi

Serves 4

1½ tablespoons
white-wine vinegar

70 ml (2¼ fl oz) water

1 teaspoon white peppercorns

4 egg yolks

210 g (7½ oz) unsalted butter at
room temperature, diced

sea salt

juice of ½ lemon

2 bunches asparagus,
bases trimmed

This dish heralds spring for many French food lovers. Asparagus was adored by Louis XIV, the 'Sun King', and soon became popular across the country. Particularly prized is the white variety that is grown in the Loire Valley.

Mastering a good hollandaise is one of the best things you can do. With its creamy texture and fresh note added by the vinegar and lemon, it's a perfect match not only with asparagus and other steamed or boiled vegetables, but also with poached eggs as 'eggs benedict', with poached chicken or fish, or with smoked salmon.

Combine the vinegar, water and peppercorns in a small saucepan and bring to a simmer. Cook until reduced by one-third. Strain into a large bowl, discarding the peppercorns, and leave to cool.

Whisk the egg yolks with the reduced liquid. Place the bowl over a saucepan of simmering water and continue to whisk until pale and foamy.

Start whisking in the butter piece by piece, adding the next one when the last one is well incorporated. After a while the sauce will start to emulsify and thicken, and you can begin adding 2–3 pieces at a time. When all the butter has been added, remove the bowl from the heat, season to taste with salt and whisk in the lemon juice.

While you are making the sauce, put the asparagus on to steam for 2–3 minutes, until tender.

Place the asparagus on serving plates and drizzle with the sauce.

THE ORCHARD

THE ORCHARD

Over an early morning breakfast in a temple of great food – the Les Halles Market in Lyon – the man referred to as the 'father of modern French cooking', Paul Bocuse, extolled the delights of France: 'It's a vineyard, a vegetable garden and an orchard … What better place in the world could you possibly choose to be a chef!'

France produces some of the most exceptional fruit in the world – apples, cherries, apricots, berries, grapes, pears, quinces, persimmons, peaches, plums, lemons, nectarines, figs and melons. There are special varieties grown in particular regions, and like great wines, some fruits have the AOC symbol – the *Appellation d'Origine Contrôlée*. This sets them apart, certifying where they are from and that they have complied with strict rules governing their cultivation (see page 13).

In Corsica, the beautiful Mediterranean island that is part of France, the air in the cooler months of November and December is scented with the fresh citrusy aroma of clementines. This is a small, intensely orange fruit, a cross between a mandarin and an orange, which is extremely juicy and highly perfumed. The Corsican clementine is considered the best in the world. They're delicious fresh, candied or preserved in syrup, and are made into aromatic liqueurs and wines. The growing, packaging and marketing of these clementines is quality-controlled, including leaving a pair of leaves attached to each fruit to show it has been picked by hand.

Back on the mainland in October, it's picking time for the famous walnuts of Grenoble. The pretty trees grow high on the hills across the Dauphiné area and three varieties – the franquette, mayette and Paris – all have AOC status. In fact, *'noix de Grenoble'* were the first fruit or nut to gain AOC status in 1938, and are always eagerly awaited as an essential part of Christmas and winter. The rules dictate that the fresh walnuts have a natural humidity above 20 per cent, are easily detachable from the kernel, and have a slight bitterness.

Walnuts are also grown in Périgord and are under the same controls – the trees must be well spaced, with a minimum distance of 7 metres (23 feet) in between, and a total area of 80 square metres (860 square feet) around each tree once it reaches its fifteenth year. This all adds up to well cared-for trees producing the best possible fruit.

In the Limousin region, the golden delicious apple has AOC status – by law the apples must be slightly elongated in shape with firm white flesh, a crisp texture, and a perfect balance of sugar and acid.

In nearby Normandy the apples are also exceptional. The orchards have been cultivated for hundreds of years and the fruit is made into the fiery apple spirit calvados and also cider – 'Normandy Champagne' according to Normandy-born chef Philippe Mouchel. Fresh apples are baked into endless beautiful desserts, with the tarte tatin being one of the most loved.

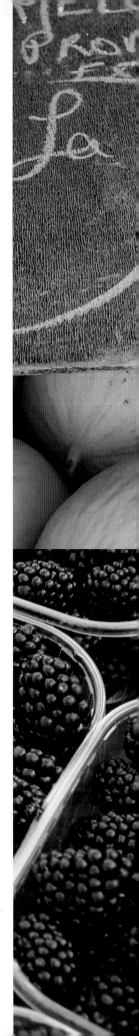

'UN DÉJEUNER DE SOLEIL.'

(Lovely but fleeting; lunch in the sun.)

In the Ardèche, a pocket of the Rhône-Alpes region in south-east France, chestnuts grow in abundance and are roasted on glowing braziers in every small town and village during the cooler months. This is the time when cakes and desserts using the new season's chestnut flour are baked. There are several chestnut varieties, and we discovered there is even a chestnut brotherhood that organises events during the season.

The list goes on – other prized fruits are the white table grapes *chasselas de Moissac* with their unusual honey-like flavour, and the black *muscat du Ventoux* grapes. The hand-harvested bunches of *muscat du Ventoux* must be a minimum weight of 250 grams (9 ounces), and the grapes must have their bloom intact without speckles, in order to qualify for AOC status.

In a charming farmhouse in Périgord, we spent a delicious morning with chef Dany Chouet as she prepared a flan with succulent prunes from nearby Agen. She soaked the prunes in armagnac, and they were cooked in a rich custard filling scented with orange-blossom water and vanilla. The history of prunes in France goes back to the twelfth century when Crusaders brought trees back from expeditions in Syria. Soon a new variety was grafted called the ente plum, which is regarded as the best plum for drying as the prunes are plump and full of flavour – perfect eaten just as they are, paired with meats, or made into desserts.

France's strict agricultural controls are undoubtedly a reason why the country excels in exceptional produce. For people living in France it creates a lifetime of great food moments, with childhood memories born from the delight of finding the first fruit of the season. For Guillaume Brahimi, nothing compares to the short *fraises des bois* or wild strawberry season. 'Just walking the streets of Paris with a punnet of those – my favourite moments!' he says. As for making dessert with them – 'You put them on a plate. That's it. The taste is unique, intense, and no other strawberry in the world comes close.'

Many homes in France have at least one fruit tree. 'Traditionally people love to plant them,' says Guillaume. 'Can you imagine how good it is to have something like a fig tree – they're simply a perfect fruit.' Those fruit trees, together with family vegetable gardens, have always allowed the French to eat well without spending too much. That subsistence has been turned into an art form with exquisite recipes for fruit flans and tarts, pies and jams, even brandies, liqueurs, schnapps and fortified wines like crème de cassis, which is made from blackcurrants.

The seasonal calendar always dictates what is available. 'In France you only find fruit in season, so you eat and cook according to the season,' explains Guillaume. 'In France you only find good melons just for a couple of months a year – they smell so good, your nose tells you where they are in the market!'

TARTE BOURDALOUE

PEAR AND ALMOND TART
from Pierrick Boyer

Serves 8–10

Sweet shortcrust pastry

250 g (9 oz/1⅔ cup) plain
(all-purpose) flour, sifted

200 g (7 oz) unsalted butter at
room temperature

80 g (2¾ oz/⅓ cup) caster
(superfine) sugar

pinch of salt

3 egg yolks

Poached pears

400 g (14 oz) white sugar

500 ml (17 fl oz/2 cups) water

2 star anise

5 cardamom pods, cracked

4 firm-ripe pears, peeled,
quartered and cored

Frangipane

40 g (1½ oz) unsalted butter at
room temperature

40 g (1½ oz) caster (superfine)
sugar

40 g (1½ oz) ground almonds

1 small egg

2 tablespoons pouring
(single/light) cream

This tart is said to have been created by a Paris pâtissier named Coquelin at his patisserie on Rue Bourdaloue. It's a perfect combination of autumn flavours, interpreted here by Melbourne pâtissier Pierrick Boyer and adapted for home cooks. Pierrick uses pears poached in syrup fragrant with cardamom and star anise. Divine!

To make the pastry, put the flour, butter, sugar and salt in an electric mixer fitted with a paddle and begin mixing. (Alternatively, you can mix in a bowl with your fingers, rubbing the butter into the dry ingredients.) Once well incorporated, add the egg yolks and mix to a dough. Shape into a disc, cover in plastic wrap and chill in the refrigerator for 1 hour.

To poach the pears, combine the sugar, water and spices in a medium saucepan and bring to the boil, stirring until the sugar dissolves. Reduce the heat to a simmer and add the pears. Poach for about 15 minutes, until tender, then remove from the syrup and leave to cool.

Butter a round tart tin about 22 cm (9 in) in diameter (alternatively you could use a rectangular tin). Place the pastry on a lightly floured work surface and roll out to 3–4 mm (⅛ in) thick. Roll the pastry around your rolling pin, then lift it onto the tin and unroll the pastry. Press the pastry into the base and side of the tin and trim off the excess pastry.

Preheat the oven to 170°C (340°F). To make the frangipane, combine the butter and sugar in a bowl and stir well. Stir in the ground almonds, then the egg, then the cream.

Spoon the frangipane into the uncooked pastry shell. Arrange the poached pears over the top. Bake the tart in the oven for around 45 minutes, or until the pastry and frangipane are golden brown.

To serve, brush the top of the tart with a little leftover syrup from the pears.

'COUPER LA POIRE EN DEUX.'
(To compromise; cut the pear in two.)

POACHED PEACHES WITH SABAYON

from Guillaume Brahimi

Serves 6

400 g (14 oz) white sugar

500 ml (17 fl oz/2 cups) water

6 large firm-ripe peaches
(white peaches are
particularly beautiful)

Sabayon

6 egg yolks

75 g (2¾ oz/⅓ cup) caster
(superfine) sugar, or more to taste

250 ml (8½ fl oz/1 cup) Marsala,
port, sherry or madeira

lemon juice (optional)

When peaches are in season, they need very little done to them to make a magnificent dessert. Here they are simply poached in syrup then peeled to reveal the rosy hue beneath their skins, and served with an elegant sabayon.

One of the delights of visiting an old-style French restaurant is when they make sabayon in front of you. It is like the zabaglione of Italy – egg yolks are beaten with wine and sugar over gentle heat to a light and foamy mousse, a perfect addition to the peaches.

Put the sugar and water in a medium saucepan and bring to the boil, stirring until the sugar dissolves. Reduce the heat to a simmer and add the peaches. Poach for 5–10 minutes, until tender, then remove from the syrup and leave until cool enough to touch. Peel the peaches and leave to cool completely.

Make the sabayon a little while before serving. Put the egg yolks and sugar in a bowl set over a saucepan of gently simmering water (a stainless steel bowl is great because of the rapid transfer of heat). Whisk briefly to combine, then slowly pour in the Marsala or other alcohol while you continue whisking. Whisk for 5 minutes or more, until the mixture has warmed and tripled in volume to a light mousse (the whisk should leave a trail as you move it through the sabayon). Whisk in drops of lemon juice or extra sugar to taste and remove from the heat. Make sure the sabayon doesn't get too hot or the eggs can curdle. Serve the sabayon warm, or leave to cool briefly, spooned over the peaches.

MINI RASPBERRY TARTS

from Guillaume Brahimi

Sweet shortcrust pastry

150 g (5½ oz) unsalted butter at room temperature, diced

80 g (2¾ oz) icing (confectioners') sugar

35 g (1¼ oz/⅓ cup) ground almonds

1 egg

1 vanilla pod, seeds scraped

250 g (9 oz/1⅔ cups) plain (all-purpose) flour

Crème pâtissière

125 ml (4 fl oz/½ cup) milk

½ vanilla pod, seeds scraped

2 egg yolks

1½ tablespoons white sugar

2 teaspoons plain flour, sifted

1 teaspoon cornflour (cornstarch), sifted

125 ml (4 fl oz/½ cup) pouring (single/light) cream

500 g (1 lb 2 oz) raspberries

icing sugar to dust (optional)

If you've ever wanted to make those little tarts that you see at the best patisseries, which look as though they're studded with jewels, then here is a simple recipe for you – perfect mouthfuls of delicious custard cream and fresh raspberries.

Combine the butter, icing sugar and ground almonds in a large bowl and mix with your fingers until well combined. Add the egg, vanilla seeds and flour and mix to a dough. Press into a ball and cover with plastic wrap. Chill in the refrigerator for at least 20 minutes and as long as overnight.

Butter 24 mini tart tins of about 4 cm (1½ in) diameter. Roll the pastry out to 5 mm (¼ in) thick on a lightly floured work surface. Use an upside-down tart tin to cut out 24 circles of pastry. Place the circles in the tins and press gently to extend the pastry up the sides of the tins. Place the tarts on a tray and chill in the refrigerator for 30 minutes while you make the crème pâtissière.

Combine the milk and scraped vanilla pod and seeds in a medium saucepan and heat gently until hot. Meanwhile, whisk the egg yolks and sugar in a large bowl until pale. Add the flours and whisk well. Gradually pour over the hot milk, whisking all the time, then return the mixture to the saucepan and place over medium heat, whisking constantly for 5 minutes, or until thick. Remove from the heat and push the mixture through a fine sieve into a clean bowl to remove the vanilla pod and any lumps. Make sure you scrape all the vanilla seeds from the bottom of the sieve back into the custard. Cover with plastic wrap and refrigerate until cold.

Preheat the oven to 170°C (340°F). Bake the tart shells for 10 minutes, or until golden. Leave to cool to room temperature.

Whip the cream to soft peaks, then fold it into the cold crème pâtissière.

Spoon or pipe the crème into the cooled pastry shells. Top the tarts with a generous amount of raspberries sitting upside-down in the crème. Dust with icing sugar if desired.

LEMON SORBET

from Guillaume Brahimi

Makes 1 litre (34 fl oz/4 cups)

about 2 lemons
440 g (15½ oz/2 cups) white sugar
500 ml (17 fl oz/2 cups) water

Sorbets (sherbets) are ancient delicacies originating in China and eventually coming to France via the Italians. Made with snow, they were popular in the French court to refresh the tastebuds as one of the courses in a feast. This classic lemon recipe is so easy and fresh-tasting, it will be your standby right through the warmer months. For lime sorbet, use the zest of three limes and the same amount of juice.

Cut off the zest of 1 lemon in thin strips. Julienne or dice the zest, and place it in a saucepan with the sugar and water. Bring to the boil, then reduce the heat to medium and simmer for 5 minutes. Remove from the heat, strain out the zest and leave to cool.

Juice the lemons until you have 125 ml (4 fl oz/½ cup) of juice. Stir into the cooled syrup, then transfer to an ice-cream maker and churn according to the manufacturer's instructions.

If you don't have an ice-cream maker, you can freeze the mixture in a bowl for 1½ hours. Remove from the freezer and stir well with a fork or beat with electric beaters, then return to the freezer. Repeat this every hour for another 3 hours or so (the more times you mix the sorbet, the smoother and lighter the results). After the last mix, transfer the sorbet to a container with a lid.

'THE TABLE IS THE PROCURESS OF FRIENDSHIP.'
French proverb

TARTE AU CITRON

LEMON TART

from Jean-Michel Raynaud and Pierre Charkos

**Sweet Shortcrust Pastry
(page 242)**

6 eggs

**350 g (12½ oz/1½ cups) caster
(superfine) sugar**

4 lemons, zested and juiced

**125 g (4½ oz) unsalted butter at
room temperature**

Lemon tarts are found in every French patisserie and can be made with other citrus, too, such as orange or mandarin or even the Japanese yuzu, which Jean-Michel adores for its complex flavour reminiscent of lemon, grapefruit and mandarin combined. This lemon filling is beautifully tangy with the butter helping to carry the flavour and adding creaminess.

Butter 5 small tart tins about 11 cm (4½ in) in diameter (or alternatively you can use 1 large tin 23 cm/9 in in diameter). Place the pastry on a lightly floured work surface and roll out to around 3 mm (⅛ in) thick. Cut circles of pastry larger than the tins and lay inside each tin, pressing the pastry into the base and sides. Trim off the excess pastry. Place the tart shells on a tray and chill in the refrigerator for 15 minutes.

Preheat the oven to 190°C (375°F). Cover the tart shells with baking paper and fill with pastry weights, rice or beans. Bake for 8–10 minutes, then remove the paper and weights and continue baking for a further 5 minutes, until lightly golden. Leave the tart shells to cool briefly while you make the filling. Lower the oven temperature to 150°C (300°F).

Put the eggs, sugar, lemon zest and juice, and butter in a blender or food processor and blend until smooth. Pour into the tart shells and bake for about 45 minutes, until the filling is just set. Allow to cool completely before removing from the tins to serve.

'SUCCESS IS THE SUM OF A LOT OF
SMALL THINGS DONE CORRECTLY.'

Fernand Point, 20th century chef and restaurateur

RASPBERRY SOUFFLÉ

from Vincent Gadan

Makes 4 individual soufflés

freeze-dried raspberry powder

500–750 g (1 lb 2 oz–1 lb 11 oz) raspberries

1 tablespoon water

50 g (1¾ oz) caster (superfine) sugar

1 heaped teaspoon cornflour (cornstarch)

juice of 1 lemon

4 egg whites

125 g (4½ oz) icing (confectioners') sugar to dust

rose petals to serve

Once mastered, this beautifully light dessert with intense raspberry flavour will be in your repertoire of special dinners for years to come. You might even feel like investing in individual copper pots that are the perfect size for soufflés, which is what pâtissier Vincent Gadan uses.

Vincent says people should be seduced by their first mouthful: 'You firstly have to think about the ingredients – the first bite of the soufflé has to be as light as possible, very flavoursome, and most importantly memorable so that the flavour lingers.' Freeze-dried raspberry powder is available at specialist cooking stores or online. As an alternative to using raspberry powder, you can simply coat the dishes in sugar.

Butter 4 individual soufflé dishes, coating well. Add a generous sprinkle of freeze-dried raspberry powder to each dish and tilt the dishes until the powder covers the butter.

Reserve 12 fresh raspberries for decorating the soufflés. Put the rest in a blender and blend to a purée. Sieve the purée and measure out 170 g (6 oz).

Put the water and 30 g (1 oz) of the sugar in a saucepan and heat, stirring, until the sugar dissolves. Mix the cornflour with the lemon juice in a small bowl and add to the sugar syrup along with 170 g (6 oz) of raspberry purée. Bring to the boil and cook for around 30 seconds, until the mixture thickens. Remove from the heat and leave to cool.

Preheat the oven to 200°C (400°F). Start whisking the egg whites – either by hand or with an electric mixer. Whisk to soft peaks, then add the remaining sugar and keep whisking to a firm meringue.

Whisk a spoonful of the egg whites through the cooled raspberry mixture until thoroughly combined. Use a spatula to gently fold the raspberry mixture through the bowl of remaining egg whites until there is no egg white visible.

Spoon the mixture into the dishes, filling right to the top. Tap the dishes gently to remove any air pockets, and smooth the tops.

Place the soufflés in a deep dish and fill with cold water to halfway up the sides of the dishes. Bake in the oven for 10–12 minutes, until well risen and lightly golden on top.

Immediately dust the soufflés with icing sugar and decorate the tops with the reserved fresh raspberries and a rose petal on each. Serve with the remaining raspberry purée, breaking the surface of your soufflé to pour it in. Enjoy!

PÉRIGORD PRUNE FLAN

from Dany Chouet

Serves 10–12

Filling

500 g (1 lb 2 oz) large prunes, stones removed

hot mild tea for soaking the prunes (if needed)

1 tablespoon armagnac (or brandy)

3 eggs plus 1 egg yolk

2 tablespoons caster (superfine) sugar

2 tablespoons cornflour (cornstarch), sifted

300 ml (10 fl oz) pouring (single/light) cream

1–2 tablespoons orange-blossom water

½ teaspoon vanilla extract

Sweet shortcrust pastry

250 g (9 oz/1⅔ cups) plain (all-purpose) flour

60 g (2 oz) ground almonds

40 g (1½ oz) caster sugar

pinch of salt

175 g (6 oz) unsalted butter at room temperature

1 egg

drop of vanilla extract

Dany Chouet was one of the pioneers of French food in Australia, opening the minds and tastebuds of several generations at her restaurants in New South Wales before she headed home to the beautiful Périgord where she was born, settling in a centuries-old farmhouse. This tart uses the famous plump prunes from nearby Agen with their shiny black skins and soft amber-coloured flesh. Dany removes the stones the day before and soaks the prunes in fragrant armagnac. They are baked in a pastry shell in custard scented with orange-blossom water and vanilla.

If the prunes are dry, soak them in tea for about 1 hour, or until soft. Drain well, then toss with the armagnac and leave to marinate overnight.

To make the pastry, combine the dry ingredients in a large bowl and mix with your fingers. Add the butter, rubbing it into the flour until the mixture is crumbly and well combined. Add the egg and vanilla and continue to mix with your hands.

Tip the mixture onto a floured work surface and press into a ball without kneading. Flatten into a disc, cover with plastic wrap and chill in the refrigerator for 20 minutes.

Butter a 27 cm (11 in) tart tin. Roll out the pastry to around 3 mm (⅛ in) thick and larger than the tin. Roll the pastry around your rolling pin, then lift it onto the tin and unroll the pastry. Press the pastry into the base and sides of the tin, and fold down the edges to create a double thickness of pastry around the sides. Cover the pastry shell with foil and pour pastry weights, rice or beans into the foil to weight down the pastry. Chill in the refrigerator for around 30 minutes, until the pastry is firm.

Preheat the oven to 200°C (400°F). Bake the pastry shell for 10 minutes, then remove the foil and weights and bake for a further 10 minutes, or until lightly golden. If any cracks or holes appear, you can patch them with leftover scraps of pastry.

Reduce the oven temperature to 180°C (350°F). Combine the eggs, egg yolk and sugar in a bowl and whisk together. Whisk in the cornflour, followed by the cream, orange-blossom water and vanilla.

Scatter the prunes inside the pastry shell. Pour the cream mixture over the top. Bake in the oven for 20–30 minutes, or until the filling is golden and just set.

The flan is best served slightly warm.

'MI-FIGUE, MI-RAISIN.' (NEITHER ONE THING
NOR ANOTHER; HALF FIG, HALF RAISIN.)

CREPES SUZETTE

from Laurent Branover

Makes 10–16 crepes

Crepes

250 g (9 oz/1⅔ cups) plain (all-purpose) flour

50 g (1¾ oz/¼ cup) caster (superfine) sugar

pinch of salt

3 eggs

500 ml (17 fl oz/2 cups) milk

2 tablespoons citrus-flavoured liqueur such as Cointreau, Grand Marnier or curaçao

butter for frying

Suzette butter

150 g (5½ oz) butter at room temperature

180 g (6½ oz) caster sugar

1 orange, zested to give fine shreds

3 sugar cubes

1 lemon

2 tablespoons cognac

2 tablespoons citrus-flavoured liqueur

To flame

2 tablespoons cognac

2 tablespoons citrus-flavoured liqueur

1 tablespoon caster sugar

Crepes are a family favourite in France and are often part of a weekend breakfast. This classic recipe is more dessert than breakfast, with lashings of citrus-flavoured butter and a finishing touch of flamed citrus liqueur.

You might like to slip some segments of orange into the crepes when you fold them up to add an extra citrus dimension.

Combine the flour, sugar and salt in a large bowl and make a well in the centre. Add the eggs and start whisking with the flour. Slowly add the milk and whisk until smooth. Add the liqueur and leave the batter to rest for 1 hour.

To make the suzette butter, combine the butter, caster sugar and orange zest in a bowl and mix well. Rub the sugar cubes against the skin of the lemon to absorb its flavour. Place the cubes in a separate bowl and add the juice of half the orange. (The remaining orange and lemon can be juiced for another purpose.) Crush the sugar cubes with a fork, mixing them into the juice. Stir the juice into the butter along with the cognac and liqueur.

Heat a crepe pan and add a small knob of butter. Add a ladleful of crepe batter, tilting the pan to spread it out to a thin crepe. Cook until golden at the edges, then flip and cook the other side. Continue cooking crepes until you have used all the batter.

Add a knob of suzette butter to the pan and when it melts (without colouring), place a crepe in the pan and coat it in the butter. Flip the crepe to coat the other side in butter, then fold the crepe in half, and in half again to a triangle. Keep the crepe warm and repeat with the rest of the crepes.

To flame the crepes, return all the folded crepes to the pan and pour on the cognac and liqueur. Carefully flame by tilting the pan towards the stove flame or by setting a match to it. Sprinkle the sugar on the flame and serve. (You can also flame each serve individually if you prefer.)

CHERRY CLAFOUTIS

from Guillaume Brahimi

Serves 4

120 g (4½ oz) ground almonds

30 g (1 oz) cornflour (cornstarch)

200 g (7 oz) caster (superfine) sugar

pinch of sea salt

4 eggs plus 2 egg yolks

2½ tablespoons pouring (single/light) cream

60 g (2 oz) butter, melted and cooled

28 cherries, pitted

icing (confectioners') sugar to dust

Vanilla Bean Ice-cream (page 227) to serve

There is no better way of celebrating the rich, dark beauty of fresh cherries than in a simple clafoutis – a pastry-less flan studded with fruit that is served hot from the oven, ideally accompanied with the best vanilla ice-cream. Guillaume's recipe has ground almonds in the batter, and his tip is to pour it over the cherries after you've put the dishes on the shelf in the oven, so you're not trying to steady full dishes of runny mixture.

Preheat the oven to 170°C (340°F). Combine the ground almonds, cornflour, sugar and salt in a bowl and mix well.

Whisk the eggs and egg yolks in a separate bowl. Continue whisking while you add the cream and melted butter. Gradually add the almond mixture, whisking constantly until thoroughly combined.

Lightly butter 4 shallow individual dishes of around 12 cm (5 in) diameter (alternatively you could use 1 large shallow dish). Divide the cherries evenly between the dishes. Ladle the batter over the cherries, filling to near the top of the dishes. Bake in the oven for 10 minutes, or until the batter is no longer sticky when tested with a skewer or knife.

Allow the clafoutis to cool slightly, then dust with icing sugar and serve with scoops of vanilla bean ice-cream.

TARTE TATIN

CARAMELISED APPLE TART

from Guillaume Brahimi

Serves 8–10

110 g (4 oz) unsalted butter

300 g (10½ oz) white sugar

7 firm apples, peeled, halved and cored

Puff Pastry (page 241)

This famous tart is upturned to reveal the season's best apples caramelised in butter and sugar, the aromatic juices seeping into the pastry base. Legend has it that the ingenious recipe attributed to nineteenth-century hotelier and cook Fanny Tatin was made by accident.

Melt the butter in a 25–28 cm (10–11 in) tarte tatin tin (or alternatively an ovenproof frying pan) over medium heat. Sprinkle in the sugar and cook without stirring until the mixture starts to caramelise. Stir gently and continue cooking until the caramel is deep golden. Remove from the heat.

Arrange the apples cut-side up in circles in the caramel, packed as tightly as possible as they will shrink during cooking. (Don't worry if the butter seems to separate from the caramel as it cools.) Return the tin or pan to medium heat and cook for about 8 minutes, until the juices from the apples start to run. Turn the heat up to high and cook until the apples have caramelised to deep golden underneath and most of the juice has evaporated. Turn each apple and continue cooking until deep golden on the other side. Remove from the heat.

Preheat the oven to 200°C (400°F). Roll out the pastry to about 2 mm (1/16 in) thick and cut out a circle a little bigger than the top of your tin or pan. Roll the pastry onto your rolling pin, then place on top of the tin or pan and unroll the pastry over the apples. Tuck the edges down around the apples. Make a small hole in the centre of the pastry to allow steam to escape.

Bake in the oven until the pastry is golden (20–25 minutes). Let the tart cool for at least 10 minutes before flipping it onto a serving plate.

'RAISSONNER COMME UNE CASSEROLE.'

(To not think logically; reason like a saucepan.)

BISTRO AND BOUCHON

BISTRO AND BOUCHON

On a rainy Friday night in the narrow cobblestoned streets of Lyon, there are gales of laughter erupting from a number of little restaurants. They're all lit with the same golden light and full of the most delicious cooking smells. Not surprisingly, everyone wants a seat inside, and many have customers lining up waiting for tables.

This type of restaurant is found only in Lyon in the city centre – it's called a *bouchon* and is an unpretentious worker's cafe that has been going strong since the sixteenth century. There are about twenty or so left, all of them once canteens for local silk workers.

The food served at *bouchons* is inexpensive, with serving sizes the opposite of haute cuisine, as this is hearty fare to sustain you. Each *bouchon* is presided over by a patron – usually male and voluble; someone who remembers regulars and their tastes, including the wine they like (which isn't too hard with only a few types served in carafes). There is no written menu as the patron either tells you what's on offer or it is scrawled on the mirrors that line the wooden interiors.

Yves Rivoiron is the patron of the Café des Fédérations, a man with a cheeky grin and a loud voice, who wears ties that are even louder with illustrations of pigs in compromising situations. 'The patron calls the shots in a *bouchon*,' he explains. 'In a restaurant the client's always right. Not in a *bouchon*! In a *bouchon* we indulge the clients – they don't even need to order. The food comes, the wine comes. It's just like home really … Except that you have to pay!'

Lyon's *bouchons* serve food that is distinctly Lyonnaise – from a simple frisée (curly endive/chicory) salad scattered with walnuts and tossed in blue-cheese dressing, to the classic lentil salad, 'the caviar of the poor', of puy lentils dressed with vinaigrette. Main courses are made with what have traditionally been low-cost ingredients – offal (variety meats), certain types of fish, vegetables. Favourites are *tablier de sapeur* (crumbed and pan-fried tripe), calves' feet and heads, chicken liver, lamb's brain, pike, cardoons and silverbeet (Swiss chard).

More widely spread across France are bistros. There is no more popular place to eat and drink than these down-to-earth establishments bustling with activity and brisk service. The tables are close together and the menu is limited, changing with the seasons.

Bistros are said to have come into being during the Russian occupation of Paris in 1815, when soldiers were in need of a quick meal and drink. The Russian word '*bystra*' means 'hurry'. These origins are disputed, but in any case bistros

are one of the delights of travelling through France, their food both wonderful and unfussy. We spent time with top chef Yves Camdeborde, who trained in some of the highest Michelin-starred restaurants in France before he decided a move to a more relaxed style of dining that was simply more fun. His bistro Le Comptoir in Saint-Germain, Paris, was at the time of writing still the hottest ticket in town, booked out months in advance.

Yves explains that a real bistro must be run by a chef. 'Because in a bistro what matters is the dish. It's a place where we make quality food that has a chef's stamp, a creator's cuisine, at a price (importantly) that is affordable for most people.'

Bistros don't have the stuffiness of fine dining, says Yves. 'Most of all a bistro is a place where you feel at ease; where there's no code. Haute cuisine is amazing in France. Thanks to my training in that, I became who I am. In such restaurants there's a code. A dress code, a speech code, a code of behaviour,' he explains. 'A bistro is a place where you live. There's life!'

The thirst for great food paired with a vibrant atmosphere is growing among starred chefs (and their chefs), who are opening bistros and turning away from the constraints and extreme pressures of the chase for Michelin stars. Yves Camdeborde is one of several examples in Paris – and the public have answered, queuing for hours in the middle of winter in the hope of getting a table.

Dining at a bistro, you can expect simple dishes done to perfection – a great steak, roast chicken or pan-fried fish with salad, bread and a glass of wine. The world changes hue as you savour the moment and leave just enough room for dessert.

'THE FRENCH ALONE UNDERSTAND COOKING, BECAUSE ALL THEIR QUALITIES – PROMPTITUDE, DECISION, TACT – ARE EMPLOYED IN THE ART. NO FOREIGNER CAN MAKE A GOOD WHITE SAUCE.'
Nestor Roqueplan, 19th century journalist

JAMÓN CROQUE MONSIEUR

from Guillaume Brahimi

thick slices of good-quality
white bread such as sourdough

unsalted butter

thin slices of beaufort or gruyère

thin slices of jamón ibérico

freshly ground white pepper

This classic ham and cheese toasted sandwich is a winner for breakfast – or as a snack mid-afternoon or late at night, or at any other time of day. Guillaume has made it bigger, better and more lavish using slabs of the best sourdough, beaufort or gruyère cheese, and the finest Spanish ham (jamón ibérico) in lieu of authentic French ham. He toasts the sandwich in the oven for the maximum melt on the cheese and a gorgeously crisp exterior.

Preheat the oven to 200°C (400°F). Butter each slice of bread and turn half the slices butter-side down on a tray. Cover these with a layer of cheese and jamón, then repeat the layers. Season with pepper. Top with the remaining slices of bread (butter-side up). Place the tray in the oven and bake the sandwiches for 15 minutes, or until the cheese is melted and the bread is golden and crisp.

'IN COOKING, AS IN ALL THE ARTS,
SIMPLICITY IS THE SIGN OF PERFECTION.'
Maurice Edmond Sailland (aka Curnonsky), 20th century food writer

RABBIT TERRINE

from Romeo Baudouin

Serves 10–12 as an appetiser

300 g (10½ oz) boneless rabbit meat, diced

100 g (3½ oz) rabbit livers, cleaned and diced

300 g (10½ oz) trimmed pork cheek, diced

300 g (10½ oz) skinless pork fat (ideally from the loin), diced

18 g (¾ oz) sea salt

2 g (⅛ oz) freshly ground black pepper (about 1 teaspoon)

1 tablespoon armagnac

1 tablespoon white wine

100 g (3½ oz) French shallots, finely diced

¼ bunch flat-leaf (Italian) parsley, finely chopped

¼ bunch tarragon, finely chopped

¼ bunch chervil, finely chopped

¼ bunch chives, finely chopped

100 g (3½ oz) egg whites (from 3–4 eggs)

6 thin slices of lardo or pancetta (optional)

100 g (3½ oz) caul fat

Glaze

5 gold gelatine leaves

250 ml (8½ fl oz/1 cup) Chicken Stock (page 250)

Make this delicious terrine as a starter and your guests will be thrilled. The secret according to charcutier Romeo Baudouin is to have the right balance of lean meat and fat in the mixture, and also to weigh out the meats after you have trimmed them to ensure you have the right ratio of mixture to salt. Full of flavour with armagnac, wine, shallots and herbs, the terrine is fabulous served with cornichons and good sourdough.

Combine the rabbit, liver, pork cheek, pork fat, salt, pepper, armagnac and wine in a large bowl. Leave to marinate in the refrigerator overnight.

The next day, push the meat through the coarse plate of a mincer (grinder) into another large bowl. Add the shallots and herbs and mix well with your hands, then mix in the egg whites.

Preheat the oven to 200°C (400°F). Line the base of a terrine dish with the lardo or pancetta, if using. Take handfuls of the meat mixture and throw them into the terrine from a short distance, to ensure the meat goes into the dish without any air pockets (which can oxidise the terrine). Continue doing this until you have put all the meat in the terrine. Use damp hands to smooth the top of the terrine and slightly mound it up like a loaf of bread. Cover the terrine with a layer of caul fat, trimming the fat to just bigger than the dish. Tuck the edges of fat down the sides of the terrine to thoroughly encase it. The caul fat helps to keep the shape of the terrine.

Place the terrine in a deep dish and bake in the oven until the top has nicely coloured to brown (about 20 minutes). Pour boiling water into the dish to surround the terrine and come halfway up the side, and reduce the oven temperature to 100°C (210°F). Bake until the internal temperature of the terrine reaches 75°C (170°F) when tested with a meat thermometer (about 2½ hours). Leave the terrine to cool.

To make the glaze, soak the gelatine leaves in a bowl of cold water for 5–10 minutes. Bring the stock to the boil in a saucepan. Take the gelatine from the bowl, squeeze out the excess water, and stir into the hot stock until dissolved. Leave to cool until the mixture starts to thicken and set, then pour over the terrine. Refrigerate the terrine for 24 hours before serving in slices with cornichons and crusty bread.

STEAK TARTARE WITH POMMES GAUFRETTES

from Guillaume Brahimi

Serves 4

320 g (11½ oz) beef tenderloin, diced into small 5 mm (¼ in) cubes or slightly larger 1 cm (½ in) cubes as desired

2 teaspoons capers, chopped

5 cornichons, finely diced

3 French shallots, finely diced

½ bunch chives, finely chopped

2 tablespoons finely chopped flat-leaf (Italian) parsley

1 teaspoon dijon mustard

3 tablespoons tomato sauce (ketchup)

3 teaspoons worcestershire sauce

dash of Tabasco sauce

1 teaspoon cognac or brandy

1 egg yolk

sea salt and freshly ground black pepper

2 large potatoes (a floury variety such as russet or spunta)

vegetable oil for deep-frying

handful of baby herbs

handful of young salad leaves

1 tablespoon Shallot Vinaigrette (page 62)

This Paris bistro dish of finely minced (ground) or diced raw beef mixed with ingredients such as capers, cornichons, shallots and herbs, and often served topped with a raw egg yolk, is named after the Tartar people of Central Asia and became popular in the early twentieth century.

Guillaume says the biggest compliment you can pay a bistro is to order their steak tartare, as it means you trust the quality of their meat. He likes to serve his tartare with *pommes gaufrettes* – potatoes sliced into thin wafers using a lattice blade on a mandoline, deep-fried to crisp perfection. They provide a crunchy base for each mouthful of delicious meat.

Combine the beef, capers, cornichons, shallots, chives, parsley, mustard, sauces, cognac or brandy and egg yolk in a large bowl. Mix until the beef is well coated. Season to taste with salt and pepper.

Peel and finely slice the potatoes using a lattice blade on a mandoline. Pour enough vegetable oil for deep-frying into a heavy-based saucepan and heat to 170°C (340°F). (If you don't have a thermometer, drop in a cube of bread when the oil seems hot – if it browns in about 20 seconds, the oil is ready.) Deep-fry the potato wafers in batches for around 1 minute each, until lightly golden. Drain on paper towel.

Dress the baby herbs and salad leaves with the shallot vinaigrette.

To serve, take a large spoon of tartare. Use another spoon to carefully scoop the tartare from the first spoon, turning the meat and shaping it as you go. Keep transferring the meat from spoon to spoon until you have a neat, smooth, torpedo-shaped quenelle, then place on a serving plate. Continue making quenelles for each plate. Arrange a small stack of potato wafers and a small mound of salad beside each quenelle.

LENTIL SALAD

from Guillaume Brahimi

Serves 4–6

500 g (1 lb 2 oz) puy lentils

5 French shallots, finely diced

4 celery stalks, finely diced

2 carrots, finely diced

a few thyme sprigs

1 bunch tarragon, leaves
picked and chopped

3 tablespoons grapeseed oil

2 tablespoons cabernet
sauvignon vinegar

sea salt and freshly
ground black pepper

pale celery leaves picked
from the inside of a
bunch, to garnish

This salad is so easy anyone can do it; so good you'll make it over and over. You dice the vegetables roughly to the size of the lentils and boil them all together, then dress them with a vinaigrette that is bright with the aniseed flavour and aroma of fresh tarragon.

Place the lentils, shallots, celery, carrot and thyme in a medium saucepan and cover with water. Bring to the boil, then reduce the heat to a simmer and cook for 20 minutes, or until the lentils are tender. Drain and transfer to a bowl.

Combine the tarragon, oil and vinegar in a small bowl. Mix well and season to taste.

Fold the vinaigrette through the lentils and vegetables and taste for seasoning. Garnish with celery leaves to serve.

'METTRE SON GRAIN DE SEL.'

(To add one's opinion; add a grain of salt.)

Charcuterie

Along with visits to the butcher, baker and cheese monger, the charcuterie is an essential stop for most French food lovers. The products of the charcutier include hams, sausages, pâtés, terrines, rillettes, confits and more. These can be snacks, party starters, delicious little interludes or the basis of light meals, and are an important part of the French diet.

The city of Lyon is renowned for its charcuterie. At the Les Halles Market, long loops of *saucisson* (salami) are strung above the shops. There are salads of pork products from snouts to ears that are lunch delicacies; tiny little sausages the size of cherry tomatoes; and golden brioche loaves cut to reveal a sausage baked inside, so all you have to add is a garden salad.

Like many other parts of French cuisine, terroir is considered an important element of charcuterie – where and how the animals are raised, the climate in which the meats are cured and the methods used.

In the Ardèche, part of the Rhône-Alpes region in south-east France, we visited a family charcuterie business that had been running for five generations. Many of the workers were the grandchildren and great grandchildren of the founders, and the methods used had not changed. A layer of fat mixed with local chestnut flour was still used in curing the hams, and the famous *saucisson* hung on the same huge racks.

The Teyssier factory is set on a plateau at 1000 metres (3280 feet) elevation, surrounded by dense pine forests. Over the years the family has purchased the forests so the pure pine-scented air can always give its distinct character to their cured meats.

The charming Stéphane Teyssier pointed out that even the same pork cured 50 kilometres (31 miles) away would taste quite different. 'It's the air and the *savoir-faire*,' he told us (the '*savoir-faire*' referring to the skills of the loyal workers).

In Australia, Romeo Baudouin is one of a small number of professional charcutiers. He trained as a chef before taking on the challenging but rewarding craft. 'I learnt from my cousin in Brittany,' Romeo told us. 'Our family have a great love of food and my cousin taught me the skills of the charcutier – passion, and commitment because it's extremely hard work. It has long hours, is labour intensive and you need to be precise ... [You need to] be able to feel the meat – "tactile" is the word I use to describe it. You need a good sense of touch.'

Romeo believes that 'charcuterie is at the root of French culture. It's a social food we like to share with friends.' Below are some common charcuterie items – perfect served on a board with crusty bread, cornichons, mustard, an onion compote perhaps, and a salad of frisée (curly endive/chicory).

Rillettes: Made from pork, rabbit, duck or any other type of poultry cooked in its own fat and then finely shredded, potted and served cold as an hors d'oeuvre. Romeo says the flavour and texture are unbeatable: 'When you put it in your mouth it's very gentle and smooth; you know, it just melts.'

Saucisson: The word 'saucisson' generally refers to cured, dried sausage (salami), while 'saucisse' refers to fresh sausage. *Saucisson Lyonnaise* is a thick, straight sausage made of pure pork with the traditional addition of truffle. The meat is marinated with cognac for forty-eight hours, then made into sausage with the addition of small squares of fat. It's matured for twelve hours then poached in stock. *Saucisson de Paris* is a classic thick pork sausage with garlic that is smoked and then poached. *Saucisson sec* is a pure pork salami with whole black peppercorns.

Jambon de Bayonne: This is the French version of prosciutto, being an air-dried salted ham from the south-west of France. Other French hams include *jambon de Paris*, which is a wet-cured ham.

Duck liver pâté: Pâtés are one of the easier charcuterie products to make at home, usually beginning with sautéing onion or shallots in butter, then browning the livers briefly. Pâtés are usually flavoured with herbs and wine or brandy (often cognac or armagnac) and are processed to a velvety consistency. Chicken livers make a slightly more delicate pâté.

Terrine: This is usually made with pork and pork fat, but can also be made with chicken, chicken liver, duck, veal, or rabbit and other game. The meat can be minced (ground), chopped coarsely or cut into strips. It is generally marinated in alcohol and mixed with herbs, spices and egg, then pressed into a loaf-shaped terrine dish and baked in the oven in a bain-marie (water bath). Terrines are served at room temperature cut into slices.

Confit: A cooking method that is usually used for duck legs, beginning with seasoning and then slow cooking in a bath of duck fat. Fully submerged and left to cool in the fat, confit is a kind of preserve. The meat is rich and melting and is a traditional ingredient of cassoulet, although duck confit can also be eaten warm on its own with potatoes, or in a salad such as with croutons, frisée and lentils.

CARAMELISED PORK BELLY

from Stéphane Reynaud in *365 good reasons to sit down to eat*

Serves 6

1.2 kg (2 lb 10 oz) piece of pork belly

sea salt

bouquet garni of bay leaves and sprigs of parsley, thyme, rosemary and sage (tied together with string)

2 tablespoons honey

2 tablespoons white port

1 teaspoon fennel seeds

1 teaspoon ground cumin

1 teaspoon coarsely ground black pepper

Stéphane makes this moist and tender pork by first gently poaching the pork in water with a bouquet garni. He then transfers the pork to the oven and transforms the skin into the best crackling on earth with honey, port, fennel seeds and cumin – it smells and tastes heavenly and the recipe is marvellously foolproof. Serve with any potato dish and roast vegetables or salad.

Use a sharp knife to score the skin of the pork in a crisscross pattern. Place in a deep saucepan and sprinkle with a generous pinch of salt. Add the bouquet garni and cover the pork with water. Place a lid on the saucepan and bring to a simmer, cooking the pork for about 1 hour, until tender (the meat should start to come away from the bones). Drain the pork.

Preheat the oven to 200°C (400°F). Combine the honey, port, fennel seeds, cumin and pepper in a bowl. Place the pork skin-side up on a rack set over a tray and spoon most of the marinade over the skin. Roast for around 15 minutes, basting a few times with extra marinade, until the skin is caramelised. Carve into thick slices and serve.

'THERE IS NO SUCH THING AS A PRETTY GOOD OMELETTE.'

French proverb

115 BISTRO AND BOUCHON

BIFTEK

THE PERFECT STEAK
from Guillaume Brahimi

sirloin, rump or fillet
steaks weighing around
200 g (7 oz) each, 2–2.5 cm
(¾–1 in) thick, at room temperature

olive oil

sea salt and freshly ground
black pepper

unsalted butter

Maître d'Hôtel Butter
(page 246) to serve

A great steak, perhaps accompanied by a well-dressed green salad (page 62) and golden *Pommes Frites* (page 52), is a meal many of us crave once in a while – simple French bistro cooking done to perfection. Cooking a good steak is about timing, but you can also tell when it is cooked by feel. Steak is cooked to medium–rare when the meat feels slightly springy when you press on it, giving a bit of resistance. A rare steak, on the other hand, feels soft and yields to the touch, while a well-done steak feels firm.

Heat a heavy-based frying pan over medium–high heat. Add a thin layer of oil to the pan and heat to hot. Season the steaks with salt and pepper on each side and place in the pan with 5 g (¼ oz) butter per steak. Reduce the heat slightly and cook the steaks for around 3 minutes on the first side. Have a look underneath to check that the meat is beautifully browned and caramelised, then turn the steaks and begin cooking on the other side for approximately 3 minutes, basting the meat with the butter and oil in the pan. If the pan seems to be getting too hot, turn the heat down a little. To tell if the meat is cooked to medium–rare, check for drops of juice forming on the surface. The meat should also feel slightly springy when you push your finger on it, giving a bit of resistance.

Lift the cooked steaks onto a warmed tray or plate and leave to rest for a few minutes. Serve each steak topped with a round of maître d'hôtel butter.

SALADE NIÇOISE

from Damien Pignolet in *Salades*

Serves 6

3–4 eggs

8 medium tomatoes,
cut into 2 cm (¾ in) slices

sea salt

1 garlic clove, bruised

freshly ground black pepper

2 green capsicums (bell peppers),
finely sliced

2 Lebanese (short) cucumbers,
peeled if desired, finely sliced

large handful of lettuce
leaves such as cos (romaine)
lettuce, torn (optional)

4 spring onions (scallions), white
part only, finely sliced diagonally

120 g (4½ oz) small black olives,
rinsed

250–300 g (9–10½ oz) good-quality
tinned tuna in oil, drained
and flaked

10 good-quality anchovy
fillets, cut lengthways into
2 or 3 thin slivers each

12 basil leaves

Vinaigrette

120 ml (4 fl oz) extra-virgin olive oil

2 teaspoons tarragon
vinegar or banyuls vinegar
(or more to taste)

sea salt and freshly ground
black pepper

An exquisite combination of some of the best ingredients from Provence. Sometimes green beans, broad (fava) beans, artichokes or potatoes are added. Damien says to use the highest-quality tinned tuna in oil as it's full of moisture and flavour, and to toss the salad gently and caressingly.

Bring a saucepan of water to the boil. Gently prick the rounded ends of the eggs with a pin (to help prevent cracking) and carefully add them to the boiling water to cook for 8–10 minutes. Refresh thoroughly under cold water, then peel and quarter the eggs.

Lay the tomato slices across a colander and sprinkle with salt. Leave to drain for 15–20 minutes, then gently pat the tomatoes dry with paper towel.

Mix the ingredients for the vinaigrette, adding the vinegar, salt and pepper to taste.

Rub a large bowl with the bruised garlic clove and season the bowl lightly with salt and pepper. Add the tomato, capsicum, cucumber, lettuce (if using), spring onion, olives, tuna and anchovies. Gently tear the basil leaves on top. Pour the vinaigrette over the salad and toss gently with your fingers to anoint the ingredients evenly with vinaigrette.

'IN FRANCE, COOKING IS A SERIOUS ART
FORM AND A NATIONAL SPORT.'
Julia Child

Butter

If there's a single ingredient you'd associate with French food, it has to be *beurre* – butter. When asked about the secrets of fine French cooking, Auguste Escoffier said there were three – 'butter, butter and butter'.

It's no exaggeration to say there is an extraordinary amount of butter used in French cooking. There doesn't seem to be a part of the kitchen without it. It's essential in puff pastry, creating all those delicate crisp layers; is added in vast quantities to mashed potato to transform it into velvety, golden heaven; and is used to start or finish sauces. When Guillaume Brahimi cooks his perfect Roast Chicken with Truffle and Cauliflower (page 144), he grabs a knob of butter to anoint the skin just as it is becoming beautifully golden. What is he doing? 'Polishing it,' he says with a twinkle.

France has two officially recognised butter-producing areas under the *Appellation d'Origine Contrôlée* (AOC) – in Normandy (this butter is labelled *d'Isigny*) and Poitou-Charentes (including the labels Échiré, Lescure and others). These distinctive, first-class butters must be naturally cultured and churned using traditional techniques, and there are versions flavoured with local sea salt.

From Brittany, another rich dairying region nearby, comes Mr Butter – the charming Jean-Yves Bordier, a superstar artisan who takes his craft a step further by flavouring, shaping and adjusting the moisture content and level of curing of his butter. He loves the product because it's truly natural: 'Butter, made with the milk from the cow – the only thing you have added is salt – it's a naturally excellent material; sensual; elegant.'

The French relationship with butter is intimate and begins with breakfast, explains Jean-Yves. 'It's the time for a slice of crusty bread with butter on top – it's the start of the day so it has to be the best possible.'

Jean-Yves flavours his butter with unusual tastes – there's yuzu butter with the Japanese citrus, which has a refreshing taste that is a great match for fish; butter flavoured with seaweed from Brittany that goes well with scallops; and butter made with fragrant espelette chilli, which is magnificent with mashed potato, a rib-eye of beef or a leg of lamb.

Jean-Yves' butter is served in top restaurants, and again he says it has to be the best. 'It's the first thing on the table – you can't disappoint!

So fundamental is butter to life in France that many everyday expressions refer to butter:

Mettre du beurre dans les épinards – To be living a little more comfortably (literally, 'To put the butter in the spinach')

Avoir un oeil au beurre noir – To have a black eye (literally, 'an eye with black butter')

Compter pour du beurre – Counts for nothing (literally, 'Counts for butter')

Vouloir le beurre et l'argent du beurre – To want it all (literally, 'To want the butter and the money for the butter')

Promettre plus de beurre que de pain – To promise much but deliver little (literally, 'To promise more butter than bread')

Faire son beurre – To make money (literally, 'To make one's butter')

Ne pas avoir inventé le fil à couper le beurre – To not be very clever (literally, 'To not have invented the wire to cut the butter')

La tartine tombe toujours du côté beurré – Murphy's law (literally, 'The bread always falls buttered side')

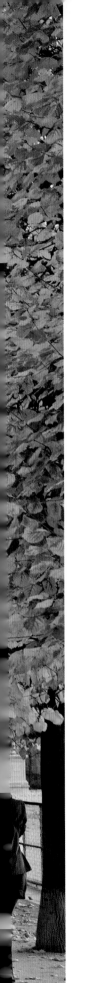

PARIS MASH

from Guillaume Brahimi

Serves 4–6

600 g (1 lb 5 oz) desiree or other all-purpose potatoes

sea salt

200 ml (7 fl oz) milk

250 g (9 oz) unsalted butter, diced

This is potato heaven and wickedness itself. Guillaume's signature mash contains a spectacular quantity of butter, but making it perfect comes down to the technique – for the potatoes to absorb all that butter, they need to be peeled while steaming hot. Take a tip from the chefs in Guillaume's kitchen, who all stop what they're doing to peel the potatoes together – use a tea towel (dish towel) to save your hands from being burnt by steam.

Boil the potatoes whole in a large saucepan of salted water until tender. Drain and peel while hot, protecting your hand by holding each potato in a tea towel (dish towel). Pass the potatoes through a food mill or push them through a fine sieve back into the empty saucepan.

Bring the milk to a simmer in a small separate saucepan. Meanwhile, stir the mash over low heat for 3–5 minutes to remove excess moisture (this will also add air to the potatoes, making them light and fluffy). Stir in the hot milk a little at a time, then do the same for the butter. The finished mash should be smooth, light and creamy.

'TO ME, BUTTER IS THAT TARTINE WITH BLUEBERRY JAM; IT'S THE AFTERNOON SNACK WITH CHOCOLATE; IT'S THE FINISH OF A SAUCE. CERTAIN RECIPES SIMPLY CANNOT BE MADE WITHOUT BUTTER.'
Guy Savoy

RIB EYE OF BEEF WITH PARIS POTATOES

from Guillaume Brahimi

Serves 3–4

1 large wagyu rib eye steak
on the bone weighing around
1.2 kg (2 lb 10 oz) (or a standing rib
roast of the same weight), brought
to room temperature

olive oil

sea salt

½ garlic bulb, sliced in
half through the cloves

1 bunch thyme

1 branch of bay leaves,
leaves picked

Paris potatoes

9 desiree or other
all-purpose potatoes

60 ml (2 fl oz/¼ cup) olive oil

3 small French shallots,
trimmed and peeled

45 g (1½ oz) unsalted butter

2 thyme sprigs, leaves picked

1 tablespoon finely chopped
flat-leaf (Italian) parsley

sea salt

Guillaume loves the decadence of cooking an enormous wagyu rib eye steak on the bone that's in excess of 1 kilogram (2 lb 3 oz), to serve several people. It's a showstopper of a steak that will spoil you for anything less. He browns it on the grill then transfers it to the oven, and one of his secrets is 'the Guillaume massage' of garlic, bay leaves and thyme.

This recipe will also work nicely for a standing rib roast with a few ribs attached. Both are perfect served with Maître d'Hôtel Butter (page 246) and Salad (page 62). Guillaume includes his recipe for Paris potatoes.

Preheat the oven to 220°C (430°F). Heat a barbecue or large frying pan to very high heat. Rub the rib eye with oil and season with salt. Rub the cut side of the garlic pieces over the meat, then bunch together the thyme and bay leaves and do the same. Set the garlic and herbs aside and place the rib eye on the hot barbecue or in the pan and brown on both sides (or brown all over if you are cooking a rib roast).

Transfer the rib eye to a tray and massage with the garlic and herbs again. If you are cooking a steak, place the garlic and herbs on top of the meat and roast in the oven for around 20 minutes for medium–rare – the meat should feel slightly springy when you press on it, giving a bit of resistance. If you are cooking a rib roast, put the meat on top of the garlic and herbs and roast for around 40–45 minutes, reducing the temperature to 180°C (350°F) after the first 15 minutes. Rest your steak or rib roast for 15 minutes before serving.

While the meat is cooking, make the Paris potatoes. Peel the potatoes and use a melon baller (also called a Parisienne scoop) to scoop balls from each potato, dropping the balls into a saucepan of cold water. Bring the saucepan to the boil, then immediately drain the potatoes.

Heat the oil in a large frying pan over medium heat and add the potato balls and shallots. Sauté, shaking the pan occasionally, until golden and cooked through. Drain off the oil (save it for another dish if desired), then stir in the butter. When the butter is bubbling and has coated the potatoes, stir in the thyme, parsley and salt to taste and toss briefly before removing from the heat.

Carve the rested steak or rib roast and serve with the potatoes, along with a salad and a round of maître d'hôtel butter on top of the meat if desired.

THE RESTAURANT

THE RESTAURANT

The restaurant is an essential part of French life, a place where one can give oneself up entirely to the very best in eating and drinking. Guillaume Brahimi describes the appeal as the sheer sensual pleasure of being looked after – and for him as a chef it's also a perfect way to see what other chefs are creating.

The modern restaurant has only developed in France over the past two hundred years. Before that, inns and guesthouses provided basic food for travellers, while taverns served wine. Meals were sustenance rather than anything artistic or truly delicious.

The French Revolution at the end of the eighteenth century abolished the system of guilds, which had meant that pâtissiers must serve pastry, rôtisseurs roasted meat, and charcutiers cured meats, without any overlap between the trades. Afterwards it became legal for establishments to serve anything they wanted, and restaurants similar to what we know today started to form. It meant that ordinary people could now access and enjoy the range of French cuisine, not just people wealthy enough to employ their own cooks.

Early restaurants specialised in meat essences or broths – called 'restaurants' coming from the word for 'restore'. From that base chefs started expanding their repertoires and eventually started getting creative.

In the mid-twentieth century a style known as nouvelle cuisine emerged, where chefs began to make strong breaks from traditional cooking methods. Dishes became fresher and more refined, with reductions preferred over heavy roux-based sauces. Chefs really started to give dishes their own stamps.

Trends in food continue to come and go, many heralded by restaurants and chefs labouring to master innovative techniques and find new ingredients. The current trend? According to Guillaume, it's a return to the classics. 'There's too much foam at the moment,' he says, referring to the molecular gastronomy movement. 'Things are not real. We need to champion real tastes – people want to know what they're eating, so that if they're eating chicken it tastes of chicken; a perfect piece of john dory tastes like john dory!'

The idea of service – being looked after – is one of the reasons many people adore the restaurant experience. And then there are those dishes that are so exceptional in the hands of a great chef, like Chui Lee Luk's take on boudin blanc (white sausage). Her version features the most delicate morsels of crab whipped with egg and cream, gently poached and served with discs of choux pastry brushed with a special mix of Asian flavours, and served with an elegant salad of asparagus, black radish and salad burnet. It's stunning food, but admittedly time

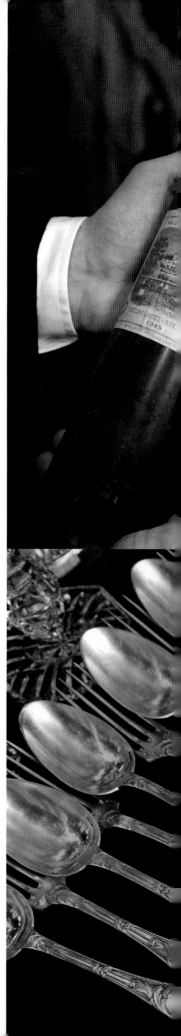

consuming. We have included a few recipes such as this in the chapter, which will be a joy and delight for experienced cooks.

The chapter also contains some classic dishes reworked into modern masterpieces, such as Shannon Bennett's chicken Grenobloise. Traditionally, 'Grenobloise' means a sauce of browned butter, capers, parsley and lemon segments, which is commonly served with fish. Shannon's steamed chicken version is light and vibrant with olive oil instead of butter, and with additions of shallots, tarragon and oregano. To finish, Shannon scatters the dish with crisp breadcrumbs, wafers of raw beetroot (beet), and egg yolks squeezed through a potato ricer, creating a dish that is a pure sensory delight.

Part of the joy of travelling through France is indulging in the French restaurant experience. *Food Safari* researcher Georgie Neal remembers arriving at one of Paris's train stations, suitcase in hand, to meet her father and enjoy lunch at one of the great restaurants – that of Joël Robuchon. 'It's the whole theatrical experience – the atmosphere, service. It's really about the details,' she says. 'You will probably go there once in a lifetime … I'll always remember that first time at Robuchon's.'

SUPRÊME DE POULET GRENOBLOISE

CHICKEN GRENOBLOISE SUPREME
from Shannon Bennett

Serves 4

8 baby beetroot (beets)

600 g (1 lb 5 oz) jersey royal or kipfler (fingerling) potatoes, or other waxy potatoes

12 radishes or baby carrots with their leaves on

4 chicken breasts

100 g (3½ oz) butter

sea salt and freshly ground black pepper

rendered chicken fat (or olive oil) for frying

200 g (7 oz/2½ cups) fresh breadcrumbs

Grenobloise

1 tablespoon finely chopped French shallot or red (Spanish) onion

1 tablespoon capers, finely chopped

1 tablespoon finely chopped flat-leaf (Italian) parsley

1 tablespoon finely chopped tarragon

2 oregano sprigs, leaves picked and finely chopped

2 eggs, hardboiled

sea salt and freshly ground black pepper

grated zest of 1 lemon and juice of ½ lemon

2½ tablespoons extra-virgin olive oil

In true form, Melbourne chef Shannon Bennett takes the dish 'Grenobloise' to a new level. Traditionally a way of cooking fish (see Snapper Grenobloise, page 189, and Trout Grenobloise, page 193), Shannon prepares it with perfectly steamed chicken and adds shallots, tarragon, oregano and hardboiled egg minced (ground) through a potato ricer to the classic salsa-like dressing. He serves this with golden potatoes fried in chicken fat, baby carrots, and crisp wafers of raw beetroot (beet) and radish – the result is fresh, inspired and incredibly delicious.

Shannon uses a steam oven to cook his chicken, but there is no problem using a large bamboo steamer over boiling water. You can also use chicken leg quarters instead of breasts (although adjust the cooking time), or even change the meat entirely as this is also a wonderful way of serving any cold meats or Christmas ham.

Put 4 of the beetroot (whole) in a small saucepan and cover with cold water. Bring to a simmer and cook until soft, then allow to cool in the water.

Put the whole potatoes in a separate saucepan and cover with cold water. Bring to a simmer and cook until they remain slightly firm as they will be pan-fried later. Drain.

While the beetroot and potatoes are cooking, prepare a bowl of water with a few drops of lemon juice. Use a mandoline to finely shave the remaining raw beetroot into the bowl, then do the same for the radishes if using, reserving the leaves for garnish. Leave in the water until ready to serve.

Begin the Grenobloise by combining the shallots or red onion, capers, parsley, tarragon and oregano in a bowl. Finely chop the whites of the eggs (or squeeze them through a ricer) and add to the bowl. (Reserve the egg yolks for garnish.)

Place the chicken breasts on a shallow dish and place inside a large bamboo steamer. Steam for 6–10 minutes, until firm to the touch. Once cooked, cover with foil to keep warm.

If using baby carrots, trim off the feathery tops of the leaves, leaving a good section of green stem. Steam until just tender. Toss with a knob of the butter and season with salt and pepper. Keep warm.

Peel the boiled potatoes and cut into thick rounds. Heat some rendered chicken fat or olive oil in a heavy-based frying pan over medium heat and add the potatoes, frying on each side until golden and crisp. If you were using olive oil, finish with a knob of butter to caramelise the potatoes. Remove from the pan and keep warm.

In the pan the potatoes were fried in, melt the remaining butter aside from a knob needed for the beetroot. Add the breadcrumbs to the pan and cook gently, stirring, until golden and crisp.

Peel the cooked beetroot and cut them in half. Reheat them in a splash of their cooking water. Finish with a knob of butter and some salt, and keep warm.

Season the Grenobloise with salt and pepper and add the lemon zest, juice and olive oil and mix well.

To serve, place the chicken breasts on one side of each plate. Lay some potato rounds on the other side and top with pieces of cooked beetroot and baby carrots (if using). Sprinkle the chicken and vegetables with toasted breadcrumbs and spoon over some of the Grenobloise. Finely chop the egg yolks (or squeeze them through a ricer) and sprinkle on top. Scatter with wafers of raw beetroot and radish (if using). Garnish with radish leaves (if using).

'EVERY MORNING THE *CUISINIER* MUST START AGAIN AT ZERO, WITH NOTHING ON THE STOVE. THAT IS WHAT REAL CUISINE IS ALL ABOUT.'
Fernand Point, 20th century chef and restaurateur

PAN-ROASTED DUCK BREAST, CONFIT DUCK LEG, KALE, AND CHERRY JUS

from Michael Smith

Serves 4

10 black peppercorns

2 juniper berries

2 garlic cloves

1 bay leaf

4 thyme sprigs

grated zest of 1 lemon

100 g (3½ oz) rock salt

4 duck leg quarters

800 ml (27 fl oz) duck fat

3 duck breasts

1 bunch kale or silverbeet (Swiss chard), stalks removed

extra-virgin olive oil

100 ml (3½ fl oz) Veal Jus (page 253)

12 cherries, halved and pitted

This classic dish from French-trained chef Michael Smith brings together the rich flavour of duck with the acidic complement of a fresh cherry sauce. Duck confit usually involves overnight salting, but Michael's recipe is a quick version that can be prepared all in the same day. His method for pan-roasting the duck breast is also cleverly simple.

Crush the peppercorns and juniper berries in a mortar, then add the garlic, bay leaf, thyme and lemon zest and crush again, releasing the flavour from the herbs. Stir in the rock salt without crushing it.

Lay the duck legs flat in a baking dish (small enough so they fit snugly) and cover with the salt mixture. Place in the refrigerator and leave salting for 1–1½ hours.

Preheat the oven to 130°C (260°F). Wash the salt from the duck legs and pat dry. Wash and dry the baking dish and return the legs to it. Heat the duck fat in a saucepan until hot, then pour it over the legs. Bake the legs in the oven for 1–1½ hours, or until the meat can be pulled easily from the bone.

When the duck legs are cooked, take them out of the fat and place on a warmed plate. Cover with foil to keep warm while you cook the remaining components.

Heat a frying pan over low heat. Season the duck breasts with salt and pepper, then place skin-side down in the pan without oil. Cook gently for about 15 minutes, until the skin is golden brown. Fat will render out as the duck cooks. Turn the heat up to medium, turn the breasts over, and cook the flesh side for 1–2 minutes, until the meat is springy to touch (indicating that it should still be a little pink inside). Transfer the breasts to a warmed plate and leave to rest for 4–5 minutes.

While the breasts are cooking, bring a saucepan of water to the boil. Once boiling, add the kale or silverbeet and blanch for 10 seconds. Drain, then put in a bowl, drizzle with a little extra-virgin olive oil, season with salt and pepper and toss to combine.

Warm the veal jus in a small saucepan and add the cherries to heat through. Slice the duck breasts.

To serve, divide the kale or silverbeet between 4 plates. Place a confit duck leg on top, and some slices of duck breast alongside. Pour over the cherry jus.

CRAB BOUDIN IN A COMPOSED SALAD

from Chui Lee Luk

Serves 4

Eggplant custard

oil

1 eggplant (aubergine)

1 egg

1½ tablespoons Champagne or Chicken Stock (page 250)

sea salt and freshly ground white pepper

splash of mirin (optional)

Crab *boudin*

350 g (12½ oz) raw crabmeat

1 tablespoon pouring (single/light) cream

1 tablespoon Fish Stock (page 250)

1 egg white

½ teaspoon Noilly Prat (dry vermouth, optional)

sea salt and freshly ground white pepper

Wafers

Choux Pastry (page 245)

2½ tablespoons light soy sauce

1 tablespoon lemon juice

1 teaspoon sugar

½ sheet of nori, cut into short, fine shreds

1 teaspoon black sesame seeds, finely chopped

1 tablespoon chicken floss

Avocado dressing

½ avocado

100 ml (3½ fl oz) Chicken Stock (page 250)

1 tablespoon Chinese rice wine

sea salt and freshly ground white pepper

Salad

asparagus, trimmed, peeled and finely sliced lengthways

black radish, skin roughly scraped, julienned

sprigs of salad burnet (or coriander/cilantro, chervil or favourite herb)

spring onion (scallion) sprouts

This masterful *salade composée* is a fusion of cuisines and techniques. Chui Lee Luk has a Malaysian background and trained in classical French cooking, including spending time with Dany Chouet who also contributes to this book. Delicate balls of eggplant (aubergine) custard and balls of crabmeat – a play on the traditional *boudin blanc* (white sausage) – are plated up with grilled slices of asparagus, julienned black radish, sprigs of salad burnet (a herb that tastes a little like cucumber), and avocado dressing. At the base of the salad is a crisp wafer of choux pastry topped with shredded nori, black sesame seeds and chicken floss. (Chicken floss is available from Asian grocers.)

Preheat the oven to 200°C (400°F). To make the eggplant custard, heat a splash of oil in an ovenproof frying pan and fry the whole eggplant until browned all over. Transfer to the oven and cook until soft.

Scoop the flesh from the skin of the hot eggplant into a sieve and gently press on it with a spoon to drain off any liquid. Purée the eggplant flesh, then pass the purée through the sieve. Measure out 90 g (3 oz) of purée (the rest can be used for another purpose) and leave to cool.

Beat the egg and pass it through a sieve to remove any foam or albumen. Mix with the eggplant purée, adding the Champagne or chicken stock. Season with salt and white pepper. Add mirin for a hint of sweetness if desired.

Place scant tablespoons of the eggplant custard on small pieces of plastic wrap. Bring the sides of the plastic up around each portion of custard, shaping into little balls, and either tie the plastic in a knot or secure with string.

To make the crab *boudin*, put the crabmeat, cream and stock in a food processor and process until smooth. Transfer to a bowl and gradually stir in the egg white. Add the Noilly Prat, if using, and season with salt and white pepper. Place scant tablespoons of the mixture on small pieces of plastic wrap and wrap as per the eggplant custard.

Bring a large saucepan of water to the boil, then reduce the temperature to just below simmering point. Drop the eggplant balls into the water and poach for about 5 minutes. Remove from the water, then add the crab balls to poach for 5–10 minutes. Remove from the water and set aside to cool.

To make the wafers, reheat the oven to 200°C (400°F). Add dollops of choux pastry dough on a tray lined with baking paper and spread them thin and wide into rough wafers. Bake for 6 minutes, then reduce the temperature to 180°C (350°F) and cook for another 6 minutes. Reduce the temperature again to 150°C (300°F) and cook for 10 minutes more, or until the wafers are crisp and golden.

While the wafers are in the oven, combine the light soy, lemon juice and sugar in a small saucepan and heat until the sugar has dissolved. Brush the mixture over the cooked wafers, then sprinkle on the nori, black sesame seeds and chicken floss. Return the wafers to the oven for a couple of minutes to dry out the dressing. Leave to cool.

To make the avocado dressing, purée the avocado, chicken stock and rice wine. Season to taste with salt and white pepper. (This dressing should be used within a couple of hours before the avocado begins to brown.)

Snip open the balls of eggplant custard and crab *boudin* and remove the plastic wrap. Lightly chargrill the slices of asparagus.

To serve, dollop a little avocado dressing onto each plate. Sit a wafer on top, anchoring it to the dressing. Add a few pieces of asparagus, julienned radish and salad burnet over and around the wafer. Dot the salad with some crab and eggplant balls, then spoon over a little more avocado dressing. Garnish with spring onion sprouts.

'THE DISCOVERY OF A NEW DISH DOES MORE FOR THE HAPPINESS OF THE HUMAN RACE THAN THE DISCOVERY OF A STAR.'
Brillat-Savarin

ROAST CHICKEN WITH TRUFFLE AND CAULIFLOWER

from Guillaume Brahimi

Roast chicken with truffle

1 × 1.6 kg (3½ lb) chicken

1 black truffle (around 50 g/1¾ oz), finely shaved

1 garlic bulb, sliced in half through the cloves

thyme sprigs

rosemary sprigs

bay leaves

45 g (1½ oz) butter

sea salt

Cauliflower, truffle and caramelised shallots

½ cauliflower, broken into florets

30 g (1 oz) butter

5 French shallots, halved

pinch of sugar

roughly chopped flat-leaf (Italian) parsley

remaining truffle from the chicken

sea salt and freshly ground black pepper

Cauliflower purée

½ cauliflower, broken into florets

500 ml (17 fl oz/2 cups) Chicken Stock (page 250)

2 tablespoons whipped cream

Get your hands on a high-quality chicken for this golden roast, fragrant with discs of truffle sitting under the skin. Guillaume 'polishes' the chicken with a knob of butter at the end of the cooking to help it attain perfection. He serves the chicken with two cauliflower side dishes – one a simple cauliflower purée and the other a dish of pan-fried cauliflower and shallots accented with a little more truffle. Inspired!

Preheat the oven to 220°C (430°F). Carefully insert your fingers between the skin and breasts of the chicken, moving all the way to the end of the breasts to create a pocket under the skin.

Place 4 or 5 large slices of truffle on each breast underneath the skin. Pull the skin back over the breasts to secure the slices of truffle. Place half the garlic inside the chicken, along with a generous bundle of thyme and rosemary and about 3 bay leaves.

Tuck the wings beneath the chicken. Truss the chicken by looping a long length of butcher's string under the chicken and around the tips of the legs. Cross the pieces of string and loop each one around the facing leg tip to pull the legs in tight to the breasts. Take the string to the back of the chicken, going underneath the wings, then around the remaining length of neck to pull the skin tight across the breasts. Tie firmly in a knot.

Rub the chicken all over with 30 g (1 oz) of the butter and season with salt. Line a roasting pan with a generous bed of thyme, rosemary and bay leaves. Nestle the remaining piece of garlic into the herbs and sit the chicken on top of the herbs and garlic. Roast for 45 minutes–1 hour, until the juices run clear. Once the chicken is cooked, rub it with the remaining butter, remove it from the pan, and cover with foil to keep warm. Take the herbs and garlic from the pan and bring the cooking juices to a simmer on the stovetop. Cook until reduced by about half.

While the chicken is in the oven, make the cauliflower dishes. For the cauliflower with truffle and caramelised shallots, bring a saucepan of water to the boil and add the cauliflower. Boil for a few minutes, then drain.

For the cauliflower purée, put the cauliflower in a saucepan with the chicken stock and simmer until soft.

Melt the butter in a frying pan and add the shallots and sugar. Fry until glossy and caramelised. Add the plain boiled cauliflower and sauté for a few minutes, letting the florets colour a little. Sprinkle with parsley and the remaining shaved truffle and season to taste. Toss for another 30 seconds before removing from the heat.

Drain the cauliflower boiled in stock, reserving the stock, and return to the saucepan. Purée with a stick blender, adding a small splash of the stock to loosen the purée if needed. Pass through a fine sieve to give a velvety texture. Stir in the whipped cream. Gently reheat the purée if needed.

Carve the chicken. Spoon some cauliflower purée onto each plate and top with the chicken. Arrange the warm cauliflower, truffle and shallot salad around the chicken. Drizzle with the reduced cooking juices.

'THE MOST LEARNED MEN HAVE BEEN QUESTIONED AS TO THE NATURE OF THIS TUBER, AND AFTER TWO THOUSAND YEARS OF ARGUMENT AND DISCUSSION THEIR ANSWER IS THE SAME AS IT WAS ON THE FIRST DAY: WE DO NOT KNOW. THE TRUFFLES THEMSELVES HAVE BEEN INTERROGATED, AND HAVE ANSWERED SIMPLY: EAT US AND PRAISE THE LORD.'
Alexandre Dumas, 19th century writer

The truffle hunt

Across the rolling hills of Périgord in south-west France, the trees are turning shades of gold and russet. It's the end of autumn and in the quiet of an oak tree grove there's the sound of a dog snuffling and his handler repeating the short sharp order: 'chercher' ('search'). Trained truffle dog Alfonse, a glossy black labrador, has his nose to the ground sniffing the soil around the base of the trees.

The truffle is a naturally occurring fungus that attaches itself to the roots of oak, hazelnut and some other trees. It's been described as an 'underground mushroom', prized for its rich and pungent aroma and flavour that adds magic to the most simple ingredients such as eggs or potatoes, transforming them into something truly exceptional.

Truffles have an earthy depth of flavour unlike anything else – they're also referred to as black gold or black diamonds, and their price makes them a definite luxury item. Luckily a little goes a long way, as one truffle, the price of which could be compared to a bottle of good French Champagne, will handsomely feed four people. (If you're fortunate you can have both and really enjoy the moment with two of the best products of France!)

As a fourth-generation truffle merchant, Pierre-Jean Pebeyre has grown up surrounded by truffles, but the autumn hunt is still exciting. He's on hand with the dog and his handler as the truffles are gathered in the field. It's just like searching for treasure, because truffles demand that a number of geographic and climatic conditions be just right. There's a real buzz as the dog's handler says 'bon chien' ('good dog') when a truffle has been sniffed and gently prised from the soil.

The Pebeyre family has a centuries-old warehouse in the town of Cahors where they pack their truffles, ready to send all over France and out to the rest of the world. They keep a few for themselves, ready for guests of course. As you'd imagine, dinner at their house is truffle heaven!

We were lucky enough to share a meal with Pierre-Jean, his wife Babé and their daughters. It started with pâté with a rich seam of finely sliced truffle, then moved on to an appetiser of the creamiest scrambled eggs liberally speckled with shavings of truffle – such a fragrant and simple start to a meal. Then, a perfectly cooked roast beef with a rich truffle sauce and the most delicious little potatoes – all served with fine Champagne. Magnifique!

SCRAMBLED EGGS WITH TRUFFLE

from Guillaume Brahimi

Serves 1–2 as an appetiser

finely shaved black truffle

3 egg yolks

unsalted butter

1 tablespoon milk

2 teaspoons whipped cream

sea salt and freshly
ground black pepper

The heady flavour of truffle works best with the simplest of ingredients such as eggs. These decadent French-style scrambled eggs are creamy and velvety – and Guillaume loves the richness of using only egg yolks. The topping of truffle elevates the dish to a classy appetiser, as we experienced at dinner with the Pebeyre family (see page 148).

To get maximum flavour from the truffle, place it in the carton with your eggs overnight to allow its aroma to permeate.

Rub the inside of a small heavy-based saucepan with butter to prevent the eggs from sticking. Whisk the egg yolks and milk in a bowl and pour them into the pan off the heat. Place over medium–high heat and stir constantly with a wooden spoon until the egg starts to thicken. Continue cooking until the egg is just set but still creamy. Remove from the heat and stir through the cream. Season to taste. Serve garnished with shaved truffle.

'TRUFFLE ISN'T EXACTLY APHRODISIAC, BUT UNDER CERTAIN CIRCUMSTANCES IT TENDS TO MAKE WOMEN MORE TENDER AND MEN MORE LIKEABLE.'

Brillat-Savarin

VOL-AU-VENT D'ESCARGOTS

VOL-AU-VENTS OF SNAILS WITH SPECK, MUSHROOMS AND PEAS IN RED-WINE SAUCE

from Robert Molines

Serves 6

600 g (1 lb 5 oz) farmed snails

Puff Pastry (page 241)

1 egg, beaten

500 ml (17 fl oz/2 cups) Beef Stock (page 253)

sea salt

100 g (3½ oz) butter

6 French shallots (or equivalent red/Spanish onion), finely diced

1 thick slice of speck, cut into batons

12 small Swiss brown or button mushrooms, quartered

4 garlic cloves, finely chopped

12 chervil sprigs, leaves picked and chopped, plus extra sprigs to garnish

300 ml (10 fl oz) red wine

80 g (2¾ oz/½ cup) freshly shelled peas

freshly ground black pepper

tiny baby carrots to garnish (optional)

Escargots – snails – have a long history in France, falling in and out of favour over the centuries. Now very popular again, the fat Burgundy snail is the most esteemed species, named because it was once prolific in the vineyards. But these snails are now protected in the wild and are mostly sourced from other parts of Europe.

There are a few snail farms in Australia, including one in Robert Molines' home of the Hunter Valley. Common garden snails are bred selectively, fed a special diet, and finally purged to clean them. The result, according to Robert, is a wonderfully nutty mouthful – delicious in a rich sauce.

Put the snails in the freezer for 1 hour to put them to sleep.

Preheat the oven to 180°C (350°F). Place the pastry on a lightly floured work surface and roll out to about 3 mm (⅛ in) thick. Cut 6 circles around 7 cm (3 in) wide to form bases for the vol-au-vents. (Alternatively, you can cut a different shape – even a snail with a large circle for its body and a head and tail at either side.) Place the pastry bases on a buttered tray and brush with the beaten egg. Cut thin rings to sit on top of the circles – they will rise and become the rims of the vol-au-vents. Brush the rims with egg and bake the vol-au-vents in the oven until risen and golden.

Pour the beef stock into a saucepan and simmer until reduced to a sauce that coats the spoon.

Meanwhile, bring a saucepan of lightly salted water to the boil and add the snails. Boil for about 15 minutes, or until they float to the surface like gnocchi. Refresh the snails briefly in a bowl of iced water, then drain. Remove the meat from each snail by stabbing it with a toothpick and pulling it out of the shell. If the snails are properly cooked, the bodies will come out easily (if not, they can break in the shell).

Heat the butter in a frying pan over low heat and sauté the shallots and speck. After a minute or so, add the mushrooms and garlic and sauté briefly, then add the snails, chervil and red wine. Once simmering, add the peas and several ladlefuls of the reduced stock and simmer until reduced to a sauce. Season with salt and pepper to taste and remove from the heat.

To serve, put the vol-au-vents on plates and spoon the snails, vegetables and sauce inside. Allow a little to spill out of the vol-au-vents onto the plates. Garnish with chervil sprigs.

BEEF CHEEK CROUSTILLANT WITH CELERIAC REMOULADE AND SAUCE VERTE

from Warren Turnbull

Serves 4

Braised beef cheeks

800 g (1 lb 12 oz) beef cheeks

1 French shallot, cut in half

1 garlic clove

1 carrot, thickly sliced

1 celery stalk, cut into
a few pieces

1 rosemary sprig

2 thyme sprigs

250 ml (8½ fl oz/1 cup) red wine

2 tablespoons port

2 tablespoons olive oil

1 litre (34 fl oz/4 cups) Veal Stock
(page 253)

Croustillant

olive oil

1 carrot, finely diced

1 celery stalk, finely diced

braised beef cheeks and some
cooking liquid

⅓ bunch flat-leaf (Italian) parsley,
finely chopped

sea salt

6–8 sheets of brik pastry

1 egg, lightly beaten

Celeriac remoulade

½ small celeriac, sliced
into fine strips

sea salt

2 tablespoons Mayonnaise
(page 257)

1 tablespoon finely chopped
flat-leaf parsley

(ingredients continue on page 157)

Beef cheeks are one of those in-vogue cuts of meat that you now see on restaurant menus. They need long, slow cooking to become meltingly tender – which is why Warren says that you put the cheeks in the oven then go to the pub for an hour or two! The braised cheeks form a soft, rich filling for elegant cigars of Tunisian brik pastry. This pastry is light and lacy, but sturdier than filo pastry, and adds a special crunchy texture ('croustillant' simply means crunchy or crisp). It's available from Middle Eastern and specialist food stores. Begin this recipe the day before by marinating the beef cheeks.

Place the beef cheeks in a dish and add the shallot, garlic clove, carrot, celery, rosemary, thyme, red wine and port. Turn the beef cheeks over in the liquid, making sure they get well coated, and leave to marinate in the refrigerator overnight.

The next day, preheat the oven to 160°C (320°F). Heat the oil in a large heavy-based, ovenproof saucepan. Take the beef cheeks out of the marinade and add to the oil, cooking until browned on each side. Pour in half the liquid from the marinade and bring to the boil. Add the vegetables and herbs from the marinade (discarding the remaining liquid) and pour in the veal stock. Return to the boil, then remove from the heat and cover the saucepan with foil. Transfer to the oven and bake for around 2½–3 hours, until the cheeks are tender enough to break up with a spoon. Take the cheeks out of the liquid and leave to cool for 30 minutes or so. Reserve the liquid.

Start the croustillant by heating a splash of oil in a frying pan. Add the carrot and celery and sauté for a few minutes. Remove from the heat before they become soft, so they retain some crunch.

Place the beef cheeks in a large bowl and break up the meat finely with a spoon or fork. Add the sautéed carrot and celery along with the parsley and 2–3 tablespoons of cooking liquid from the cheeks. Season with salt and mix well. Lay a piece of plastic wrap on a work surface and place around 3–4 tablespoons of the beef mixture on top. Roll the beef tightly in the plastic to form a sausage. Continue making another 6–8 sausages with the mixture. Chill the sausages in the refrigerator for 1 hour to firm up.

To assemble the croustillant, lay a sheet of pastry on a work surface. Add a sausage unwrapped from its plastic about a third of the way across the pastry. Brush the remaining two-thirds of pastry with beaten egg and

Sauce verte

1 bunch flat-leaf parsley,
leaves picked

½ bunch mint, leaves picked

1 French shallot, roughly chopped

1 anchovy fillet

10 capers

2 teaspoons dijon mustard

2 teaspoons chardonnay vinegar

1½ tablespoons olive oil

roll the sausage up inside the pastry. The egg should stick the pastry together. Trim off the excess pastry at the ends of the sausage. Continue rolling the remaining sausages in pastry. Refrigerate until ready to cook.

To make the remoulade, mix the celeriac and a pinch of salt in a bowl. Stir in the mayonnaise and parsley.

To make the *sauce verte*, combine all the ingredients in a blender and blend to a smooth purée.

Heat some olive oil in a frying pan and add the sausages wrapped in pastry. Fry, turning every so often, until golden brown all over.

To serve, place a spoonful of remoulade onto each plate. Next to it add a dollop of *sauce verte*. Cut the sausages in half and add 3–4 pieces to each plate, sitting them on top of the sauce.

Equipment

Kitchen equipment is a little like classic French fashion – there are endless bits and pieces, most of which are not used for months at a time. However, most French kitchens have key items that are expensive to buy initially, but come out on top with the cents-per-use equation that women use to justify the purchase of a great dress or jacket … they're good quality, used often and work every time. Here are some of the main items needed in a French kitchen:

Copper saucepans and frying pans: Like crepe pans, some families have copper cookware handed down through the generations. Copper pots and pans are considered the best conductors of heat, giving quick and even cooking.

Crepe pan: This is another investment piece – a short-sided, heavy-based pan put to use on many weekends for family breakfasts or for making desserts.

Enamelled cast-iron pot: A heavy pot that is great for slow braising and can be transferred to the oven when making casseroles.

Whisk: The French tool par excellence, for whipping cream or egg whites by hand, making sauces or mayonnaise, or mixing batters for cakes or crepes.

Knives: A chef's knife, a medium-sized knife and a small paring knife are the three main knives that are good to have. Learning how to keep them sharp is also important.

Food mill: Also called a mouli, this is a manual food processor that looks like a colander with a handle and a winder. Fantastic for puréeing tomatoes or making the finest mashed potato.

Tamis: A very fine sieve shaped like a drum that can be used for many of the same purposes as a food mill, such as making fine mashed potato and other purées and sauces. The food is pushed through the sieve using a spatula.

Chinois: A conical sieve for straining custards, sauces and other liquids, pushing out the last whispers of flavour.

Mandoline: For precision slicing and julienning, such as for wafer-thin slices of truffle or perfect matchsticks of carrot. The best mandolines prop up on a bench and have a few different blades. With a lattice blade you can make *Pommes Gaufrettes* (page 107).

BOEUF EN CROÛTE

BEEF FILLET BAKED IN PASTRY

from Serge Dansereau in *French Kitchen*

Serves 4

800 g (1 lb 12 oz) beef fillet
(centre-cut for even thickness)

sea salt

freshly ground black pepper

80 ml (2½ fl oz/⅓ cup) olive oil

100 g (3½ oz) butter

500 g (1 lb 2 oz) field mushrooms,
stems removed, peeled and
roughly chopped

4 French shallots, finely chopped

1 teaspoon thyme leaves
(or a combination of chives and
flat-leaf/Italian parsley)

12 slices of prosciutto

Puff Pastry (page 241)

2 egg yolks, well beaten
with a pinch of sea salt

Red-wine sauce

2 tablespoons olive oil

4 French shallots, finely chopped

1 onion, finely chopped

½ teaspoon white
peppercorns, crushed

½ teaspoon black
peppercorns, crushed

1 field mushroom, sliced

2 garlic cloves, finely chopped

500 ml (17 fl oz/2 cups) red wine

500 ml (17 fl oz/2 cups) Beef Stock
(page 253)

2 thyme sprigs

2 rosemary sprigs

Boeuf en croûte (called beef wellington in the United Kingdom) is one of the most spectacular dishes you can serve to a table of guests – perfectly cooked lean beef with a coating of mushroom duxelles (a kind of mushroom pâté) and prosciutto wrapped in flaky pastry, served with a rich red-wine sauce. Serge advises sourcing a quality butter puff pastry made by a pâtissier (or alternatively you can make it yourself). This is Serge's birthday dinner every July, and is perfect served with sautéed carrots and green beans.

Dry the beef fillet with paper towel then season well with salt and pepper. Heat half the oil and 15 g (½ oz) of the butter in a large frying pan over high heat. Add the beef and seal well on all sides, cooking for around 5 minutes in total. Remove to a plate and allow to cool.

Place the mushrooms in a food processor and process until very finely chopped. Heat the remaining oil and butter in the frying pan over high heat. Add the shallots and sweat for 1 minute, then add the mushrooms and cook for 15 minutes, or until all the liquid has evaporated from the mushrooms and the mixture is very dry. Remove from the heat, season to taste, and add the thyme. Leave to cool for 15 minutes.

Lay a large sheet of plastic wrap on a work surface. In the middle arrange the prosciutto slices lengthways, with each slice slightly overlapping. Spread the mushroom mixture over the prosciutto. Lay the beef on top of the mushrooms and wrap the prosciutto and mushrooms around the beef, enclosing everything in the plastic. Secure tightly and chill in the refrigerator for 1 hour to firm up.

While the beef is chilling you can make the sauce. Heat the oil in a saucepan over high heat. Add the shallots and onion and sauté for 5 minutes or until caramelised. Add the pepper, mushroom and garlic and sauté for another 2 minutes. Add half the wine and boil until nearly dry. Pour in the remaining wine and boil again, this time until reduced by three-quarters. Add the stock and bring to the boil, then lower the heat and simmer for 20 minutes or until reduced by half (skim the sauce regularly to

remove any impurities). Strain the sauce through a fine sieve into a smaller saucepan and bring back to the boil, skimming again. Simmer for a final 10 minutes, until the sauce is glossy and has the consistency of pouring (single/light) cream. Remove from the heat and add the thyme and rosemary sprigs, and set aside for 10 minutes to infuse. Strain to remove the herbs and keep the sauce warm until needed. (The sauce can be made up to 5 days in advance, stored in the refrigerator and reheated if desired.)

Preheat the oven to 220°C (430°F). Place the pastry on a lightly floured work surface and roll out to a rectangle large enough to wrap around the beef and about 3 mm (¼ in) thick. Remove the plastic from the prosciutto-wrapped beef and place in the centre of the pastry. Fold one side of the pastry over the beef and brush the edge with beaten egg. Roll the beef over, enclosing it in the pastry. Trim off any excess pastry from underneath the beef. Trim any excess pastry from the ends and tuck them under, pressing to seal. Place the parcel on a tray and brush the top with egg. Decorate the parcel with leaves cut from the pastry off-cuts, brushing these with egg also. Use a fork to draw decorative lines over the pastry. Chill the parcel in the refrigerator for 10 minutes.

Place the beef in the oven and cook for 5–10 minutes, until the pastry is golden, then reduce the temperature to 140°C (280°F) (open the door for a minute to help lower the heat). Cook for a further 20 minutes, which should give you nice, juicy, pink beef.

Rest the beef for 5 minutes, then place on a board and cut off the pastry ends. Cut the beef in half, then cut each piece in half again to give 4 thick slices. Serve on warmed plates with the red-wine sauce.

'NOTHING WOULD BE MORE TIRESOME THAN EATING AND DRINKING IF GOD HAD NOT MADE THEM A PLEASURE AS WELL AS A NECESSITY.'
Voltaire

SEAFOOD

Mouline
3€Kg

SEAFOOD

France is in a perfect position for seafood – 'the only country to be bathed by the North Sea, the Atlantic Ocean and the Mediterranean' in the words of Paul Bocuse. Paul delighted in using some of the best French produce for many decades in his restaurants in Lyon and Paris.

Walk through any fresh food market in France and the seafood stalls are a delight, smelling fresh and briny like the sea. There are creatures of all shapes and sizes – live crustaceans and every kind of shellfish, including the dark shapes of unopened oysters. 'I never saw oysters sold open before I came to Australia,' says Guillaume Brahimi. 'For us that means they are not at their absolute best.'

The range of fish on offer is dizzying – dory, red mullet, sole, sea bass, turbot, gurnard, the ugly but delicious monkfish, and the beautiful blue and silver slimy mackerel. It's all ready for the French public who covet the best there is.

At the huge wholesale Rungis International Market on the outskirts of Paris, a whole ocean is boxed up on beds of crushed ice, tended in the pre-dawn hours by men in laundered white coats. Sides of orange salmon hide under drifts of ice, while boxes of spiny black sea urchins flown in from Iceland are wheeled into position. The top is sliced off an urchin and handed to Guillaume. 'It's like swallowing a big wave!' he says after tasting the custardy and intense iodine flavour.

Live yabbies scuttle in big glass tanks, and in the next tank are langoustines (scampi) from the Brittany coast waving their claws. In crates of ice are many types of crabs and shellfish – scallops, tube-shaped razor clams, pretty sea snails, mussels, oysters, cockles, periwinkles and more.

'The thing to remember is that seafood has its seasons too,' explains Guillaume. 'You know you are better eating oysters in months finishing with the letters "*bre*" – never in June, July or August … A fish like turbot is an autumn fish, while bass and *rouget* (red mullet) are springtime.'

We were lucky enough to travel through France in autumn and discovered how extraordinary the *coquille saint jacques* (scallops) are. Their size alone is staggering – plump with shells measuring up to 15 centimetres (6 inches), and simply delicious eaten raw (perhaps sliced and served with hazelnut oil and frisée/curly endive/chicory salad) or quickly pan-fried and served as Guillaume does with leek confit and a dollop of caviar, which is a recipe we share with you in this chapter.

At Yves Camdeborde's bistro Le Comptoir in Saint-Germain, we enjoyed scallops served with generous shavings of white truffle, all bought at the market that morning. Sublime!

The other wonderful discovery of our French trip was the fantastic smoked salmon at the markets. We saw huge sides of salmon with that brilliant rosy orange colour and a gentle smoky aroma. There was wild-caught salmon from Scotland, deep-orange salmon from Norway, and more varieties from Ireland – some of the very best salmon in the world. One of our more memorable lunches while filming was sourdough baguettes with four different types of smoked salmon … This would have made a lovely picnic on a sunny day beside a river with a nice glass of wine, but as always we were racing to the next location so Guillaume assembled the baguettes on the front seat of our van. These were the best smoked-salmon rolls of our lives! Each salmon was subtly different in texture and taste, and in a way they captured what is really good about French food – simplicity and utter perfection.

BOUILLABAISSE

from Guillaume Brahimi

Serves 8

3 red mullet, cleaned and scaled

3 leatherjackets (or other mild oily fish), heads removed, skinned and cleaned

3 red rock cod (scorpion fish), cleaned and scaled

olive oil

thick strip of orange zest

1 fennel bulb, sliced

2 celery stalks, sliced

2 tomatoes, chopped

2 garlic cloves, crushed with the back of a knife

handful of thyme sprigs

3 tablespoons tomato paste

2 tablespoons fennel seeds

generous pinch of saffron threads

100 ml (3½ fl oz) Pernod

Fish Stock (page 250)

Potato rouille

500 g (1 lb 2 oz) desiree or other all-purpose potatoes

3 egg yolks

1 tablespoon dijon mustard

750 ml (25½ fl oz/3 cups) grapeseed oil

3 garlic cloves, finely chopped

generous pinch of saffron threads

sea salt

(ingredients continue on page 172)

Bouillabaisse had fairly humble beginnings as a soup cooked by fishermen in Marseilles, Provence. Fish not destined for market were boiled in a cauldron on the beach with shellfish and spices. Traditional bouillabaisse contains several kinds of fish and must include scorpion fish. Saffron, orange zest and fennel are some of the other key flavours.

Guillaume's version uses fish from Australian waters, which he chops, boils and processes – bones, head and all. The mixture is strained to give a thick, velvety purée, and then Guillaume goes to town adding scallops, mussels and crabmeat. He finishes the soup with toasted slices of baguette spread with potato rouille (this tastes marvellous even without the soup). It's a dish to pop in the middle of the table to delight all of your friends.

Use a cleaver to chop through the body of each fish at around 3 cm (1¼ in) intervals – the fish may or may not stay connected in one piece.

Heat a generous splash of oil in a pot over medium–high heat and sauté the fish (heads included) for 5 minutes. Add the orange zest, sliced fennel, celery, tomato, garlic and thyme and mix well. Stir in the tomato paste, fennel seeds, saffron and Pernod and cook for 3 minutes. Slowly pour in enough fish stock to just cover the ingredients and simmer for around 40 minutes.

While the soup is cooking, make the rouille. Boil the potatoes whole in their skins until soft. Meanwhile, sit a large mixing bowl on a folded damp cloth (to keep it stable) and add the egg yolks and mustard. Whisk well. Add a little grapeseed oil and whisk until well incorporated. Keep adding

To serve

1 baguette

500 g (1 lb 2 oz) mussels, cleaned and de-bearded

12 scallops on the half-shell

250 g (9 oz) picked crabmeat

chopped flat-leaf (Italian) parsley

small amounts of oil and whisking well after each addition. The mayonnaise should begin to thicken once about 60–80 ml (2–2½ fl oz/¼–⅓ cup) of oil has been added. Then you can start adding the oil in a thin and steady stream down the side of the bowl while you continue whisking.

When the potatoes are cooked, drain and leave to cool for a few minutes before peeling off their skins. Place in a wide bowl and mash roughly with a fork. Add the garlic, saffron and salt to taste and continue mashing to combine. Fold in the mayonnaise.

When the soup is cooked, tip the contents (bones and all) into a blender and blend until smooth. Do this in several batches if necessary. Pass through a fine sieve back into the pot, pressing out as much liquid and flavour as you can.

When ready to serve, slice the baguette thinly and toast the slices in a hot oven until crisp and golden. Return the soup to the heat and check the seasoning. When simmering, add the mussels and cook until their shells open.

Lay the scallops (raw on their shells) around the base of a large serving bowl (or in individual serving bowls). Scatter with the crabmeat. Ladle the hot soup and mussels over the top. Sprinkle with parsley. Spread potato rouille generously onto the baguette croutons and float them on top of the soup.

'NO COOKING IS GOOD IF IT IS NOT DONE OUT OF FRIENDSHIP FOR THE PERSONS FOR WHOM IT IS DESTINED.'
Paul Bocuse

SCALLOPS WITH CONFIT OF LEEK AND CAVIAR

from Guillaume Brahimi

Serves 4

200 g (7 oz) unsalted butter

4 large leeks, white part only, cut in half lengthways and finely sliced

sea salt

20 scallops on the half-shell (roe off or on as desired)

2½ tablespoons crème fraîche

juice of ½–1 lemon

freshly ground white pepper

1 tablespoon olive oil

100 g (3½ oz) caviar

chervil to garnish (optional)

Buy the best and freshest scallops on the half-shell for this standout appetiser, delicious in its simplicity. Then cook the leeks slowly in butter confit-style to release the maximum sweetness. The caviar adds a wonderfully decadent touch.

Melt the butter in a medium saucepan over low heat and add the leek and a pinch of salt. Cook very gently, without allowing the leek to colour, for 1 hour or until completely soft. Once cooked, drain off any excess butter if necessary.

While the leek is cooking, prepare the scallops. Remove them from their shells and wash gently in a large bowl of iced water. Pat the scallops dry and sit them on a tray, keeping them upright and plump. Wash and dry the shells and lay them out on a platter or on individual plates. You might like to rest the shells on a bed of salt so they lie flat.

Reheat the leek until warm if needed and stir through the crème fraîche. Add lemon juice to taste and season with extra salt (if needed) and white pepper.

Season the scallops. Heat a frying pan over high heat and add the oil when very hot. Place the scallops in the pan and fry for around 30 seconds on each side, until the surface is lightly caramelised. Remove the scallops from the pan.

To serve, place half a tablespoon of warm leek confit in each scallop shell. Top with the scallops. Garnish each with a teaspoon of caviar and a small sprig of chervil if desired. Enjoy immediately.

JOHN DORY NORMANDE

from Philippe Mouchel

Serves 4

4 large raw prawns (shrimp)

70 g (2½ oz) butter, plus extra for the dish

2 French shallots, finely diced

500 g (1 lb 2 oz) mussels, cleaned and de-bearded

100 ml (3½ fl oz) dry cider or dry white wine

100 g (3½ oz) small button mushrooms, stems trimmed

sea salt

lemon juice

4 john dory (or similar white fish) fillets, weighing about 160 g (5½ oz) each, skin on

10 g (¼ oz) butter

freshly ground black pepper

200 ml (7 fl oz) pouring (single/light) cream

1 tablespoon whipped cream

4 large oysters, shucked, juices reserved

1 tablespoon finely chopped flat-leaf (Italian) parsley

Fumet

50 g (1¾ oz) butter

1 onion, finely sliced

2 celery stalks, finely sliced

bones from 2 john dory (or similar white fish), cut into large pieces

250 ml (8½ fl oz/1 cup) dry cider or dry white wine

bouquet garni of 2 parsley stalks, 1 bay leaf and 1 thyme sprig (tied together with string)

This recipe from renowned Melbourne chef Philippe Mouchel is an ode to his home of Normandy, featuring a medley of seafood, the best butter and cream, and apple cider, which Philippe describes as 'Normandy Champagne'. Philippe starts by making a fumet – a concentrated fish stock – using the bones of the fish. If you can't find cider from Normandy, opt for another deep-coloured dry cider, or alternatively use a dry white wine.

To make the fumet, melt the butter in a large saucepan over medium heat. Add the onion and celery and sauté until the onion is translucent. Add the fish bones and pour over the cider or wine, then add the bouquet garni and bring to simmering point, skimming well. Simmer for 30 minutes, then remove from the heat and leave to rest for a further 20 minutes. Strain the fumet through a fine sieve and set aside.

Bring a saucepan of water to the boil and cook the prawns for 3–4 minutes, until their shells change colour, then drain and leave to cool. Shell them, leaving their heads and tails intact, and set aside.

Melt 50 g (1¾ oz) of the butter in a large saucepan over medium heat. Add half the shallots, the mussels and the cider or wine and bring to the boil. Cover with a lid and simmer for 5 minutes, or until the mussels open. Strain the cooking liquid through a fine sieve and set aside. Remove the mussels from their shells and set aside.

Melt the remaining butter in a small saucepan and add the mushrooms, a pinch of salt, a teaspoon of water and a splash of lemon juice. Cover with a lid and cook over medium heat for 3 minutes.

'WHEN ONE THINKS OF LA GRANDE CUISINE ONE CANNOT THINK OF MONEY; THE TWO ARE INCOMPATIBLE. LA GRANDE CUISINE IS EXTREMELY EXPENSIVE – BUT THAT DOES NOT MEAN ONE CANNOT DO VERY GOOD COOKING WITH INEXPENSIVE INGREDIENTS.'
Fernand Point, 20th century chef and restaurateur

Preheat the oven to 170°C (340°F). Butter a baking dish large enough for the fish fillets to lay flat inside (or use 2 dishes). Place the fish in the dish and dot with a little more butter. Season with salt and pepper. Sprinkle with the remaining shallots and pour on the fumet. Press a sheet of baking paper over the surface of the fish and bake for about 8 minutes, or until not quite cooked through.

Turn off the oven and open the door for a few moments to let some of the heat escape. Transfer the fish fillets to a serving dish and cover with foil. Return to the oven to keep warm while you make the sauce.

Pour the cooking juices from the fish and the reserved mussel liquid into a saucepan. Bring to the boil over moderately high heat and cook until reduced by half. Add the pouring cream and reduce until lightly thickened. Add the whipped cream, shelled mussels, mushrooms and prawns to heat through. Finally, add the oysters and their juices and a little more lemon juice.

To serve, spoon the mussels, prawns, oysters, mushrooms and sauce over the fish and sprinkle with parsley.

'LIFE IS TOO SHORT ... FOR DIETS. DIETETIC MEALS ARE LIKE AN OPERA WITHOUT THE ORCHESTRA.'
Paul Bocuse

Wine

Ask a wine buff about wine in France and the answer can be a little unexpected – the French make some of the best and worst wines on the planet. 'There's a lot of dross – *vin ordinaire* – made in France,' explains wine writer Ben Edwards. 'So much so that people visiting France can have less than great experiences with wine they think is cheap and cheerful, and it just turns out to be cheap! But then there are exceptional wines, really great wines that come from a country perfectly suited to growing grapes and from people who have meticulously sourced the right variety of grape for the climate and soil.'

Before the French Revolution, the Catholic Church owned many vineyards throughout France, especially in Burgundy and Champagne, and started thinking about the concept of terroir – the combination of climate, soil, aspect and other variables that add up to making grapes – or indeed any produce – develop a flavour that is particular to a place. Legend has it that the monks, who documented all their discoveries, actually *tasted* the soil of particular vineyards to help narrow down the best grape varieties for the area.

Chef and wine lover Tony Bilson, known as the godfather of French food in Australia, believes that the regional food of France seamlessly matches the wines of the regions because of the terroir. It balances certain characteristics of the wine with that of the food.

'The most important thing to look at in flavour profiles is acid, followed by fruit and earth flavours,' he explains. 'The acid in wine tends to put flavours in perspective. There's a hint of cabbage in the rieslings from Alsace … what do they go best with? *Choucroute* – the favourite local dish of pork and cabbage!'

Ben Edwards cites the perfect combination of duck and pinot noir: 'The fat of a duck is highly aromatic and pinot is a high-acid wine that's subtle and spicy and offsets the flavours of the duck while cutting through the fat and cleaning up the palate, ready for the next bite and sip … Or, take a high-tannin, high-acid, high-fruit cabernet from Bordeaux and put it with lamb – pungent, big flavours and a little fatty. Magnificent!'

'BURGUNDY MAKES YOU THINK OF SILLY THINGS,
BORDEAUX MAKES YOU TALK OF THEM AND
CHAMPAGNE MAKES YOU DO THEM.'
Brillat-Savarin

Other great combinations of French regional food and wine include the stew of freshwater fish and red wine (*matelote*) matching the beautiful wines of Burgundy; muscadet white wine with fresh seafood or shellfish; high-acid wines from rugged Jura in Franche-Comté, eastern France, cutting through and complementing the rich local cheeses; and bouillabaisse, the famous fish stew of Marseilles, best enjoyed with rosé.

Tony Bilson says his favourite quote about food from Auguste Escoffier also applies to wine: 'Cookery will evolve – as society itself does – without ever ceasing to be an art.'

For many of us, French wine *is* an art, with the skills of the artisan producer, the history of thousands of years, and the land itself creating sheer magic in a glass.

MOULES MARINIÈRE

MUSSELS IN WHITE WINE

from Guillaume Brahimi

Serves 4

1 tablespoon olive oil

8 French shallots, finely chopped

4 garlic cloves, crushed

125 ml (4 fl oz/½ cup) dry white wine

125 ml (4 fl oz/½ cup) Fish Stock (page 250)

2 kg (4 lb 6 oz) mussels, cleaned and de-bearded

50 g (1¾ oz) unsalted butter

sea salt and freshly ground black pepper

½ cup roughly chopped flat-leaf (Italian) parsley

This dish literally translates as 'mariner's mussels'. It relies on the freshness of the mussels as they are so simply flavoured with white wine, shallots, garlic and parsley. This is classic bistro fare – inexpensive, delicious, and easy to prepare in a busy kitchen as it only requires a saucepan.

Heat the oil in a large saucepan over medium heat. Add the shallots and sauté for 2 minutes, or until soft. Add the garlic and cook for another minute, until aromatic, then add the wine and stock. Bring to the boil, then reduce the heat to a simmer and cook for 5 minutes, reducing the liquid slightly.

Turn up the heat and add the mussels to the pan. Cover with a lid and cook, shaking the pan occasionally, for 5 minutes, or until the mussels have opened.

Tip the mussels into a colander set over another saucepan to catch the broth. Return the broth to the boil, add the butter and season to taste. Place the mussels in serving bowls and pour the broth over the top. Scatter with the parsley and serve.

'FOOD WITHOUT WINE IS A CORPSE; WINE WITHOUT FOOD IS A GHOST; UNITED AND WELL MATCHED THEY ARE AS BODY AND SOUL, LIVING PARTNERS.'

André Simon, 20th century wine writer

SNAPPER BRANDADE

from Peter Robinson

200 g (7 oz) table salt

10 g (¼ oz) kombu (dried kelp)

½ teaspoon coriander seeds, toasted and ground

grated zest of 1 lemon

1 large skinless snapper (porgy) fillet weighing about 1 kg (2 lb 3 oz)

80 ml (2½ fl oz/⅓ cup) olive oil

1 celery stalk, sliced

1 leek, finely sliced

½ fennel bulb, sliced

5 garlic cloves, crushed

1 bay leaf

1 thyme sprig

2 litres (68 fl oz/8 cups) milk

1 teaspoon black peppercorns

1 medium potato, peeled and cut into large dice

1 tablespoon chopped chives

Brandade is a purée of salt cod originating in Provence – it's *brandada* in Spain; *mantecato* in Italy. The soaked dried fish is whipped with olive oil and potatoes and served as an appetiser. In this version Peter uses local snapper (porgy) as a lighter, fresher alternative. He salts the fish for twenty-four hours with a little kombu (Japanese dried kelp), coriander seed and lemon zest, then poaches it in milk with aromatics. Serve the brandade with garlic toast and a leaf and herb salad.

Blitz the salt and kombu in a food processor. Add the ground coriander and lemon zest and blitz again briefly.

Lay the snapper fillet on a large piece of muslin (cheesecloth) and coat with the salt on both sides. Wrap in the cloth and refrigerate for 24 hours, turning at around 8 hours and again at around 16 hours.

Heat 1 tablespoon of the oil in a pot and add the celery, leek, fennel, garlic, bay leaf and thyme. Sweat until the vegetables are beginning to soften, then pour in the milk and add the peppercorns. Bring the milk to a simmer. Brush all the excess salt from the snapper and add to the milk. Poach very gently for 8 minutes, then remove the snapper to a plate and leave to cool.

Boil the potato in a small saucepan of water until soft, then drain, mash and leave to cool.

Flake the fish, removing any bones. Put into a food processor with the mashed potato. Turn on the motor and immediately begin pouring in the remaining oil in a steady stream to make a thick and creamy emulsion. Turn off the motor before the fish becomes too finely chopped.

Serve the brandade garnished with chives.

'ÇA NE MANGE PAS DE PAIN.'
(It won't hurt; it doesn't eat bread.)

SNAPPER GRENOBLOISE

from Meyjitte Bougenhout

Serves 4

1 small lemon

250 ml (8½ fl oz/1 cup) Fish Stock (page 250)

2 large potatoes, peeled and cut into thick slices

1 cinnamon stick

1 star anise

2 tablespoons olive oil

4 × 150 g (5½ oz) thick snapper (porgy) fillets, skin on

sea salt and freshly ground black pepper

4 handfuls baby spinach

15 g (½ oz) butter

handful of sourdough croutons

2 tablespoons slivered almonds

2 teaspoons capers

2 tablespoons chopped flat-leaf (Italian) parsley

8 pieces of semi-dried (sun-blushed) tomato

Meyjitte Bougenhout comes from the city of Grenoble in the French Alps, which is famed for its delicious fish dishes 'à la Grenobloise' with capers, lemon flesh, parsley and croutons. Meyjitte was one of the youngest chefs ever to receive a Michelin star in France. Later he moved to Australia, where he now has Absynthe on the Gold Coast. He likes to add semi-dried tomatoes as an extra dimension to this delicious dish. It takes less than fifteen minutes to cook and looks and tastes sensational.

Use a small, sharp knife to cut the peel and pith from the lemon. Holding the lemon in one hand and the knife in the other, cut on either side of each segment to remove wedges of flesh without pith or membranes. Slice into thin triangles.

Bring the fish stock to a simmer in a small saucepan and add the potatoes, cinnamon and star anise. Cover and cook for about 5 minutes, until soft.

While the potatoes are cooking, heat 1 tablespoon of the oil in a frying pan over medium–high heat. Score the snapper fillets with a couple of shallow cuts on the skin side, and season the flesh side with salt and pepper. Place the snapper fillets in the hot pan skin-side down. Fry until crisp (3–4 minutes), then turn the fish over, reduce the heat to low and cook for another 5 minutes. Remove to a plate and keep warm.

Add the remaining oil to the pan and quickly wilt the spinach, adding salt and a dash of fish stock from the potatoes. Remove to a bowl.

Add the butter to the pan along with the remaining ingredients, including the lemon slices and 1 tablespoon of the fish stock. Sizzle briefly, seasoning to taste.

To serve, place slices of potato in the middle of each plate. Top with the spinach and then the fish. Scatter with the ingredients from the frying pan.

DEMI-CURED KING SALMON WITH BROTH AND PICKLED VEGETABLES

from Peter Robinson

Serves 4

Bacon, kombu and bonito broth

120 g (4½ oz) bacon, diced

2 litres (68 fl oz/8 cups) water

20 g (¾ oz) kombu (dried kelp)

15 g (½ oz) bonito flakes (shavings of dried salted bonito fish)

3 teaspoons Japanese soy sauce

1 tablespoon lemon juice

Vegetable pickle

150 ml (5 fl oz) white-wine vinegar

150 ml (5 fl oz) water

1½ tablespoons honey

1 French shallot, sliced

2 teaspoons black peppercorns

1 teaspoon fennel seeds

2 cloves

100 ml (3½ fl oz) celery juice

1 purple carrot

1 yellow carrot

1 radish

⅓ long cucumber

1 celery stalk

1 candy-cane (chioggia) beetroot (beet)

Cured salmon

1 teaspoon coriander seeds

1½ teaspoons black peppercorns

900 g (2 lb) table salt

300 g (10½ oz) white sugar

grated zest of 1 lemon, lime or orange

4 × 200 g (7 oz) portions of king salmon with belly flaps trimmed for even thickness, skin on, pin bones removed

grapeseed oil

For this elegant dish pieces of salmon are part-cured, seared for crispy skin, then served in a broth with a Japanese twist. Fine slices of heirloom vegetables pickled in spiced celery juice are scattered over the top.

Make the broth and begin the vegetable pickle a day ahead.

For the broth, gently brown the bacon without oil in a large heavy-based saucepan. Add the water and kombu and gently heat to 50°C (100°F) (without a thermometer, this is water that is a little too hot to keep your fingers in). Keep the water at this temperature for 30 minutes. Then gently increase the heat and bring to a simmer, add the bonito, and remove from the heat. Leave to stand for 5 minutes before straining out the bacon, kombu and bonito. Add the soy and lemon juice to the broth and chill in the refrigerator overnight.

To make the pickle, combine the ingredients except the celery juice and vegetables in a saucepan. Bring to a simmer, then add the celery juice and remove from the heat. Leave the liquid to cool, then refrigerate overnight (adding the vegetables the next day).

The next day, prepare the cure for the salmon by toasting the coriander seeds and peppercorns in a dry pan until fragrant. Grind in a mortar, then transfer to a bowl and mix with the salt, sugar and zest. Lay the salmon pieces in a dish skin-side down and cover with the salt mixture. Leave to stand for 3 hours. Remove the salmon pieces from the salt, brushing off all the excess. Score the skin of the salmon.

Finely slice the vegetables for the pickle using a mandoline. Soak the sliced vegetables in a bowl of iced water for 5 minutes, then drain well. Strain the pickling liquid and pour into a bowl. Add the sliced vegetables.

While the vegetables are pickling, skim off any bacon fat from the surface of the chilled broth and pour into a saucepan. Gently bring to the boil.

While the broth is heating, heat a frying pan over medium heat. Add a thin film of grapeseed oil to the pan. Pat the skin of the salmon pieces dry with paper towel and place in the pan skin-side down. Sear without turning for around 5 minutes, until the skin is dark golden and crispy.

While the salmon is searing, warm 4 shallow bowls.

Drain the seared salmon pieces of excess oil and place in the centre of the warmed bowls. Pour the hot broth around the fish (it's important for the broth to have just boiled so it's hot enough to continue cooking the fish that has only been seared on one side). Garnish with slices of drained pickled vegetables and serve.

TROUT GRENOBLOISE

from Peter Robinson

Serves 4

250 g (9 oz) country-style bread

150 ml (5 fl oz) grapeseed oil

sea salt and freshly ground black pepper

2 lemons

4 small rainbow trout, cleaned and scaled

plain (all-purpose) flour

200 g (7 oz) unsalted butter

2 tablespoons capers, rinsed

handful of flat-leaf (Italian) parsley leaves, chopped

Trout is an adored fish in France, popular almost everywhere because the rivers that intersect the countryside make it easily accessible. Each region prepares the delicate fish slightly differently, and this is another delicious fish dish 'à la Grenobloise' (see Snapper Grenobloise, page 189). The trout is cooked whole and there are plenty of crunchy croutons and browned butter sauce. Peter likes to serve this with new potatoes tossed in garlic and parsley butter, and with a garden salad.

Preheat the oven to 150°C (300°F). Rip the bread into small pieces and place on a tray. Dress with half the oil and season with salt and pepper. Bake for 15 minutes, or until golden.

Use a small, sharp knife to cut the peel and pith from the lemons. Holding a lemon in one hand and the knife in the other, cut on either side of each segment to remove wedges of flesh without pith or membranes. Do the same for the other lemon.

Heat the remaining oil in a large frying pan over medium heat. Season the fish with salt and pepper and dust with flour. Fry until golden (around 4 minutes on each side). Add half the butter to the pan and heat until foaming. Briefly baste the fish with the butter, then remove the fish to warmed plates. Melt the remaining butter in the pan and stir in the capers, parsley and lemon segments. Adjust the seasoning of the mixture, then pour over the fish. Add the croutons to the hot pan to catch all the remaining butter, tossing briefly. Scatter over the fish and serve.

'THE PLEASURES OF THE TABLE BELONG TO ALL TIMES AND AGES, TO EVERY COUNTRY AND EVERY DAY; THEY GO HAND IN HAND WITH ALL OUR OTHER PLEASURES, OUTLAST THEM, AND REMAIN TO CONSOLE US FOR THEIR LOSS.'

Brillat-Savarin

FISH QUENELLES

from Philippe Mouchel in *Taste Le Tour*

Serves 2–3

250 ml (8½ fl oz/1 cup) milk

75 g (2¾ oz) butter

125 g (4½ oz) plain (all-purpose) flour

4 egg yolks, plus 1 egg white

250 g (9 oz) skinless delicate white fish such as snapper (porgy)

100 g (3½ oz) veal kidney fat (suet), finely chopped

sea salt and freshly ground black pepper

pinch of freshly ground nutmeg

300–400 ml (10–13½ fl oz) crayfish (spiny lobster) bisque

100 g (3½ oz) cooked crayfish meat, cut into small pieces

Philippe learned the art of making these light and delicate fish cakes when he worked for Paul Bocuse in Lyon. The fish mixture is scooped into elegant quenelles (torpedo-like shapes) using two spoons. The quenelles are poached in water then baked briefly in the oven in a luxurious moat of crayfish bisque.

Philippe's quenelle recipe includes a little veal kidney fat (suet) with the fish – a prized meat fat for cooking as it has a mild flavour and firm texture that allows it to be chopped rather than rendered. It gives crispness to pastry and here it makes the mixture easier to work with.

Ready-made bisque can be purchased from specialist food stores – it's a velvety soup that's a sophisticated ode to the sea.

Bring the milk and butter to boil in a medium saucepan.

Put the flour in a bowl and stir in the egg yolks. Add to the milk and whisk over the heat until the mixture thickens then comes together as a soft dough-like mass. This is called a 'panade'. Transfer to a bowl to cool.

Remove any bones from the fish and roughly chop the flesh. Place in a food processor with the egg white and blend to a purée. Add the kidney fat and blend briefly. Add the panade in small knobs and blend briefly until well combined. Season the mixture with salt, pepper and the nutmeg and blend a final time. Transfer the mixture to a bowl and chill in the refrigerator for at least 1 hour.

Bring some water to a simmer in a wide saucepan. Once simmering, start spooning quenelles into the water. To do this, take a neat, smooth scoop of fish mixture on a large metal spoon. Use another large spoon to scoop the mixture from the first spoon onto the edge of the second spoon, shaping the mixture into a neat torpedo. Carefully drop the quenelle into the simmering water. Continue making quenelles until you have used all the mixture (you should get 4–6 large quenelles). Poach gently for 6–8 minutes, then scoop from the water with a slotted spoon and drain on paper towel.

Preheat the oven to 200°C (400°F). Heat the crayfish bisque in a saucepan. Place the quenelles in individual ovenproof dishes with 2 per dish. Ladle the bisque into the dishes three-quarters of the way up the quenelles. Garnish with a little crayfish meat.

Bake in the oven for about 10 minutes, until the surface is golden.

INDULGENCE

INDULGENCE

The intricate world of French sweets is based on the fundamentals of great ingredients and skilful techniques. Often just a handful of ingredients are whipped into masterpieces that almost seem too beautiful to eat.

There could be nothing more mouth-watering than stepping into one of Paris's great patisseries such as La Grande Epicerie, Fauchon or Pierre Hermé (see page 206), all as gorgeous as any chic boutique or lingerie shop – beautifully lit with glass cases full of sweet treats to tease the eye, the aroma so good you become a little weak at the knees.

'That smell changes during the day,' explains Melbourne pâtissier Pierrick Boyer. 'You start the day with the smell of early morning croissants, and then it may change to the aroma of raspberry jam cooking out the back, or warm chocolate as the day goes by.'

Even though he spends all day surrounded by these wonderful smells, Pierrick still finds the world of the patisserie exciting and remembers getting shivers when he discovered an old-fashioned Paris bakery filled with some of the most wonderful croissants, brioche, macarons, danishes, eclairs and elaborate little cakes.

While filming in Paris, we spent quite a few early morning hours in the kitchen of Blé Sucré ('Sweet Wheat') with renowned pâtissier Fabrice le Bourdat – one of those lovely Frenchmen who seems to speak poetry when they talk about food. Fabrice worked in luxury hotels before opening his own patisserie, and says he still gets goose bumps when people confess that they love his shop and his cakes, biscuits and breads.

He told us the story of a customer asking if she could buy something and pick it up the next day. 'No, no,' was the answer. 'I will make it tomorrow for you so you can have it fresh!' Yesterday's baking simply isn't good enough. French people commonly buy desserts rather than make them themselves, and are judged by the calibre of the establishment they purchase from.

Anything in a box from Blé Sucré is prized. Fabrice's *pain au chocolat* has been voted the best in Paris, and people cross town for his madeleines, *chausson aux pommes* (apple turnover) and *pain au raisin*. On one of the early mornings we visited it was *kouign amann* being prepared, a special pastry from Brittany that consists of very flaky, caramelised discs of pastry made with enormous amounts of Breton butter. Truly 'sweet wheat' on an entirely new level!

Memories of beautiful indulgences have inspired French writers over many years. One famous piece of writing is from Marcel Proust's seven-volume opus *Remembrance of Things Past* when he tastes a madeleine served by his mother:

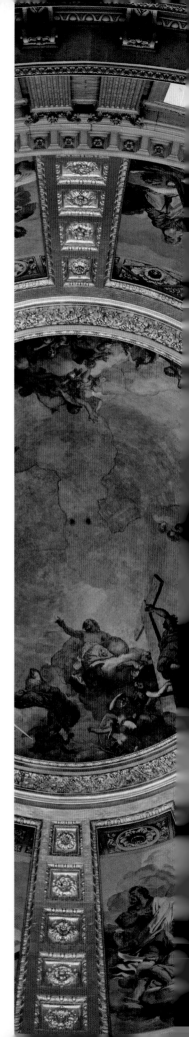

'She sent for one of those squat, plump little cakes called "*petites madeleines*", which look as though they had been moulded in the fluted valve of a scallop shell … I raised to my lips a spoonful of the tea in which I had soaked a morsel of the cake. No sooner had the warm liquid mixed with the crumbs touched my palate than a shudder ran through me and I stopped, intent upon the extraordinary thing that was happening to me. An exquisite pleasure invaded my senses …'

I wonder what Proust would have said if he had tasted the luxuriously indulgent vanilla bean ice-cream that is served in Guillaume Brahimi's restaurants – creamy, heavily perfumed and speckled with thousands of tiny black vanilla seeds. The recipe is found in this chapter. Or Vincent Gadan's luscious raspberry soufflé, sweet and slightly tart, and so light you feel angels had a hand in creating it – this recipe is in The Orchard chapter.

The moment of biting into a macaron is another heavenly experience with its combination of creamy filling and crisp meringue shell. Macarons, of course, originated in France – it's the epicentre of the macaron revolution that is sweeping the world. Jean-Michel Raynaud from the elegant Baroque Bistro in Sydney shares his signature recipe for salted caramel macarons. 'A perfect macaron – for me you need to have a nice rounded shape,' he says. 'A smooth top. Shiny. And a nice little foot. And the trick is to actually get the height of the macaron to develop nicely without having the macaron being empty inside.'

'I have now been making macarons for thirty years and never cease to be amazed by the technical challenge they can be. Whether it is a change in humidity, the type of almond you use, the size of the batch you make – any variation is bound to affect the finished product,' explains Jean-Michel. 'Every time we do a batch, I can't help but go to the oven door and look in amazement at the little foot coming out from under a beautifully shiny shell.'

Macarons have 'infinite scope for creating new fillings and colour combinations,' Jean-Michel tells us. He enjoys the challenge of creating creams that complement the shells and are able to be eaten and enjoyed without the macaron needing refrigeration.

To be a true player in the delicious and pretty world of macarons, you need artistic flair and a knowledge of the colour palette, on top of the required technical skills. 'Of course, there is something beautiful about a whole display of colourful macarons in a shop window – it just makes me happy!' Jean-Michel says.

VANILLA CRÈME BRÛLÉE

from Guillaume Brahimi

Serves 4

300 ml (10 fl oz) pouring (single/light) cream

200 ml (7 fl oz) milk

2 vanilla pods, seeds scraped

100 g (3½ oz) egg yolks (from around 5 eggs)

70 g (2½ oz) caster (superfine) sugar

30 g (1 oz) demerara sugar

'Crème brûlée' literally translates as 'burnt cream', which does nothing to highlight its sensual delights. It's a perfect mix of creamy and crunchy; a rich baked custard with a hard toffee crust that's slightly tart. You get to have fun with a blowtorch – a great present for any cooking devotee.

Preheat the oven to 130°C (250°F). Put the cream, milk and vanilla pod and seeds in a saucepan and gently bring to the boil, then remove from the heat.

Whisk the egg yolks and caster sugar in a bowl until just combined, then pour the hot cream over the top, whisking constantly. Strain the mixture through a fine sieve into a pitcher to remove the vanilla pod and any lumps, but be sure to scrape the vanilla seeds from the bottom of the sieve back into the cream. Pour into 4 × 180 ml (6 fl oz) ramekins.

Put the ramekins in a deep dish and fill the dish with hot water to halfway up the sides of the ramekins. Cover with foil and bake for 1 hour, or until the custards are set but still have a slight wobble. Remove the ramekins from the water and allow to cool for 20 minutes, then transfer to a refrigerator to chill for 4 hours, or until cold.

To serve, sprinkle the custards with the demerara sugar and caramelise using a blowtorch.

'TO RECEIVE GUESTS IS TO TAKE CHARGE OF THEIR HAPPINESS DURING THE ENTIRE TIME THEY ARE UNDER YOUR ROOF'
Brillat-Savarin

LEMON MADELEINES

from Guillaume Brahimi

40 g (1½ oz) unsalted butter

100 g (3½ oz/⅔ cup) plain
(all-purpose) flour

½ teaspoon baking powder

100 g (3½ oz) caster (superfine)
sugar

1 egg

1½ tablespoons milk

1 vanilla pod, seeds scraped

grated zest of 1 lemon

melted butter and caster
sugar for serving (optional)

These elegant cakes shaped like scallop shells are the perfect thing with a cup of light, floral French tea. Guillaume's are flavoured with vanilla bean, lemon and *beurre noisette* – butter cooked until hazelnut brown, giving a nutty flavour. Madeleine trays are available at most good cookware stores and make all the difference to the appearance; they are worth purchasing as once you've mastered these cakes you'll be making them over and over. You can have the mixture ready in advance and cook the cakes when your guests arrive so you can all enjoy warm madeleines.

Melt the butter in a small saucepan over high heat and cook until nut brown.

Sift the flour, baking powder and sugar into a bowl. In a separate bowl, whisk the egg with the milk. Pour this into the flour mixture and whisk until combined, then add the vanilla seeds and whisk again. Gradually pour in the browned butter and whisk well, then whisk in the lemon zest. Allow the mixture to rest for 1–2 hours in the refrigerator.

Preheat the oven to 170°C (340°F). Butter the madeleine moulds, coating well. Spoon or pipe the mixture into the moulds and bake for 6–10 minutes, or until golden.

Tap the madeleines out of the moulds onto a rack to cool briefly. Serve dipped in melted butter and caster sugar if desired.

'PASTRIES ARE A PROMISE OF SWEETNESS, A TANGIBLE EXPRESSION OF A PASTRY MAKER'S AUDACIOUS DREAMS. THEIR TASTES AND FRAGRANCES EVOKE MEMORIES. THE CREATIVE DIMENSION OF PASTRY MAKING MEANS THAT IT IS AN ART FORM.'

Pierre Hermé, pattisier

In the Realm of Pierre Hermé

Let me describe the moment of pushing open the glass door to one of Pierre Hermé's salons of sweets. It's a sleek and modern boutique, the centrepiece a large tangerine cabinet enclosing neat rows of jewel-like macarons and perfect little cakes – some with gold leaf shimmering atop glossy chocolate, some featuring pink discs of meringue decorated with fresh raspberries. The smell is sweet heaven with vanilla and chocolate drifting out from the kitchens behind. These kitchens are bustling with activity as fillings are piped onto cakes and mixes are swirled together. At least a hundred different delights are created in any one day.

Pierre Hermé, whose initials are repeated over and over in very smart black and white wallpaper on the ceiling, has several of these shops in Paris as well as in Tokyo and London. He's a fifth-generation baker, starting his own apprenticeship at the age of fourteen with the acclaimed Paris pâtissier Gaston Lenôtre. Ten years later he became the pastry chef at the fine-food merchant Fauchon, then at the luxury pastry temple Ladurée. Pierre was the youngest person ever to be named France's Pastry Chef of the Year, and is also the only one to have been awarded a Chevalier of Arts and Letters and later the even more prestigious Legion of Honour.

Pierre has worked to distil what he considers the perfect essence of key flavours such as chocolate, coffee, caramel and vanilla, exploring their dimensions with an almost scientific precision. 'I wanted to create my own taste of vanilla because I taste several types of vanilla from all over the world,' he explains. 'It's not one taste that I like. It's a combination of different vanillas – from Madagascar, Tahiti and Mexico. [My work] is interesting because it's not only mixing a lot of ingredients together. You can work on just one flavour, one taste.'

Pierre Hermé's vanilla tart is life changing. It's called *tarte infiniment vanille* – 'infinite vanilla' – and begins with a shortbread base. The next layer is a creamy vanilla and white chocolate ganache enclosing a lady-finger biscuit moist with vanilla syrup. On the top is a thick layer of vanilla and mascarpone cream. It's love at first bite … and that flavour combination is repeated and played out in Pierre's eclairs, macarons and other pastries. This is one of Pierre's techniques – coming up with a great flavour, then carrying it through a range of confections. 'I try a tart,

a jam, a *pain du fruit*, ice-cream, cake … and you have a lot of different products based on the same flavour combination,' says Pierre.

One of his signature flavour combinations is rose, lychee and fresh raspberries, which started initially in the form of a macaron and which Pierre now uses in other more elaborate creations called 'fetishes'. He has travelled the world for inspiration to create new and clever delights, and some of his other flavour combinations include green tea, passionfruit and chestnut; chocolate and passionfruit; and strawberry and pistachio.

'Firstly [I come up with ideas] in my head and after we taste I can improve, or sometimes it's right on the first time, but it's based on my feelings,' Pierre explains. 'Mostly you have the combinations based on my experience and my experience of taste, and because I taste everything.'

The patisserie

'The Parisian pastry chef is truly a man to be admired. Imagine his responsibility. Day in and day out, he must attend to the care and feeding of the formidable Parisian sweet tooth,' writes Patricia Wells in *The Food Lover's Guide to Paris*.

The Oxford Companion to Food defines pastries as a collection of items 'produced by the skill of the pâtissier, usually based on short, puff or choux pastry, génoise sponge, or rich, yeast-leavened mixtures of the brioche type'. Jam, cream, chocolate, *crème pâtissière* (rich, thick custard) and icing add contrasting flavours and textures, and the pastries must of course be as seductive to the eye as they are delicious. Here is a run down of some of the delights of the French patisserie:

Croissant: This crescent-shaped symbol of France is made with yeasted puff pastry and is often enjoyed for breakfast.
Pain au chocolat: Croissant dough baked with a layer of chocolate inside.
Brioche: Lightly sweet yeast bread enriched with butter and eggs, traditionally baked in a fluted tin.

Danish: Flaky yeasted pastry enriched with butter and eggs, with fruit nestled in the centre.

Eclair: Long finger of choux pastry filled with crème pâtissière or whipped cream, usually topped with chocolate icing.

Croquembouche: Translating as 'crunch in the mouth', the croquembouche is a tower of choux pastry puffs filled with crème pâtissière, each dipped in toffee to stick them together. The spectacular conical structure is often finished with spun sugar.

Religieuse: Translating as 'nun', this pastry resembles a nun in her habit. A small choux pastry puff sits atop a larger puff, both filled with crème pâtissière. The 'nun' is then coated in icing.

Saint honoré: Named after the patron saint of bakers, this cake starts with a base of pastry. Placed around the rim is a circle of choux pastry puffs filled with crème pâtissière that has been lightened with cream or beaten egg whites, with more crème filling the middle of the cake.

Paris-brest: Named after an old cycle race, this ring-shaped pastry resembles a wheel. Made with choux pastry, it is topped with flaked almonds and is split and filled with cream.

Mille-feuille: 'A thousand leaves'. Generally three sheets of flaky puff pastry are sandwiched with crème pâtissière, often with icing on top.

Pithivier: A puff-pastry pie filled with frangipane that is traditionally enjoyed at Epiphany.

Opera cake: Thin layers of almond sponge sandwiched with coffee butter-cream, finished with a glossy coating of chocolate.

Financier: Small teacakes made from a batter containing ground almonds and egg whites. Traditionally baked in rectangular shapes to resemble gold bars, but now in other shapes.

Madeleine: Small scallop-shaped sponge cakes often flavoured with vanilla and lemon.

Baba au rhum: Otherwise known as 'rum baba', this is a rich yeast bread traditionally containing rum-spiked raisins. After baking it is soaked in a rum-based syrup and is sometimes filled with crème pâtissière.

Macaron: Biscuits (cookies) made with ground almonds, egg white and sugar sandwiched together with butter cream, in a variety of flavours and colours.

PITHIVIER

from Jean-Michel Raynaud

Serves 6

Puff Pastry (page 241)

1 egg, beaten

100 g (3½ oz) white sugar

3 tablespoons water

Frangipane

125 g (4½ oz) unsalted butter
at room temperature

125 g (4½ oz/1 cup) icing
(confectioners') sugar

2 eggs

125 g (4½ oz/1¼ cups) ground
almonds

15 g (½ oz) plain (all-purpose) flour

2 tablespoons rum

100 g (3½ oz) Crème Pâtissière
(page 257)

This elegant pie filled with frangipane is traditionally made for Epiphany, celebrated on the first Sunday in January.

Sydney pâtissier Jean-Michel Raynaud from Baroque Bistro suggests it can be eaten warm with an anis custard (custard flavoured with aniseed liqueur such as Pernod) or cold with a coffee or tea.

'It is a must-have on Epiphany in France,' he remembers. 'I will never forget my first year as an apprentice making over four thousand pies over the two days leading to Epiphany. It was a traumatic experience … but I still eat them, as always, on the first Sunday of January!'

Jean-Michel's tip is that it's better to slightly overcook the pithivier.

To make the frangipane, put the butter and icing sugar in a bowl and beat to combine. Beat in the eggs one at a time, then stir in the ground almonds, flour and rum, followed by the crème pâtissière.

Place the pastry on a lightly floured work surface and roll out to a large rectangle about 3 mm (⅛ in) thick. Cut 2 circles 28 cm (11 in) in diameter (find something you can use as a stencil to cut a neat circle, such as a large cake tin).

Place one circle on a tray. Add the frangipane in the middle of the circle and shape into a neat dome leaving a distance of about 3–4 cm (1¼–1½ in) around the edges. Brush the edges with a little water and top with the second circle of pastry, pressing lightly around the edges to seal. Use a small, sharp knife to trim the edge of the circle in a small scalloped pattern so the pithivier resembles a flower with lots of small petals.

Cover the pithivier with a buttered upturned tray and flip the pithivier over from the bottom tray to the top. The underside of the pithivier should now be the top. Brush the pithivier with the beaten egg and chill in the refrigerator for 30 minutes.

Preheat the oven to 200°C (400°F). Brush the pithivier with more beaten egg, then use a small sharp knife to score a circle around the pithivier just in from the scalloped edge. Be careful not to cut all the way through the pastry. Then, score curved lines arcing out from the centre of the pithivier to the edge of the circle, fanning all the way around the pithivier. Bake the pie in the oven for 35 minutes, or until nicely browned.

While the pithivier is baking, heat the sugar and water in a small saucepan, stirring until the sugar dissolves. When the pithivier is cooked, brush it with the syrup for a glazed surface. Serve the pithivier warm or at room temperature.

COEUR À LA CRÈME D'ANJOU

CREAM HEART FROM ANJOU

from Gabriel Gaté

Serves 6–8

2 egg whites

pinch of cream of tartar

110 g (4 oz/½ cup) caster (superfine) sugar

200 ml (7 fl oz) pouring (single/light) cream

250 g (9 oz) quark

juice of 1½ lemons

600 g (1 lb 5 oz) raspberries

juice of 1 orange

icing (confectioners') sugar to dust

This delicate dessert made with fresh soft cheese is a speciality of Gabriel's native home of Anjou in France. The *coeur* or 'heart' is moulded in a special heart-shaped porcelain dish that is perforated with holes to drain off the excess moisture of the cheese. (A colander can be used as an alternative, although you won't end up with the same pretty shape.) The cheese traditionally used is fromage blanc, but quark can be used instead.

Beat the egg whites and cream of tartar to stiff peaks. Add one-third of the sugar and continue beating until smooth.

Lightly whip the cream in a separate bowl.

In a third bowl whisk the quark with another third of the sugar and one-third of the lemon juice. Fold in the whipped cream, then gently fold in the beaten egg whites.

Place a heart-shaped mould on a tray. Line the mould with damp piece of muslin (cheesecloth), then fill with the cream mixture. Cover with the muslin and drain in the refrigerator for at least 4–5 hours or overnight.

Purée half the raspberries with the remaining sugar, lemon juice and orange juice. Pass through a sieve to remove the seeds. Chill in the refrigerator.

Carefully turn the heart out onto a serving plate. Top with the remaining whole raspberries and dust with icing sugar. Serve with the raspberry sauce.

Chocolate

The French have been refining and working with chocolate for hundreds of years to create some of the smoothest, richest, most elegant chocolates in the world.

It was Italian explorer Christopher Columbus who stumbled across cacao beans in Central America in 1502. In the seventeenth century chocolate reached France, becoming all the rage in the court at Versailles during the reign of Louis XIV. He appointed Monsieur David Chaillou as the first person to make and sell chocolate in the country, ensuring the king a constant supply of the delicious substance.

Chocolate became highly fashionable throughout Europe and was declared a source of health by renowned gastronome Brillat-Savarin. 'Those who have been too long at their labour, who have drunk too long at the cup of voluptuousness, who feel they have become temporarily inhumane, who are tormented by their families, who find life sad and love ephemeral … they should all eat chocolate and they will be comforted,' he declared. Inspiring words.

In Paris, chocolate shops are some of the most seductive places to walk into – boutiques full of the heady aroma of chocolate, so beguiling one is powerless to resist.

One of the most exciting memories of our trip to France filming *French Food Safari* is of visiting the huge chocolate workshop of one of Paris's most exclusive stores – La Maison du Chocolat. We watched

'THOSE WHO HAVE BEEN TOO LONG AT THEIR LABOUR, WHO HAVE DRUNK TOO LONG AT THE CUP OF VOLUPTUOUSNESS, WHO FEEL THEY HAVE BECOME TEMPORARILY INHUMANE, WHO ARE TORMENTED BY THEIR FAMILIES, WHO FIND LIFE SAD AND LOVE EPHEMERAL; THEY SHOULD ALL EAT CHOCOLATE AND THEY WILL BE COMFORTED.'
Brillat-Savarin

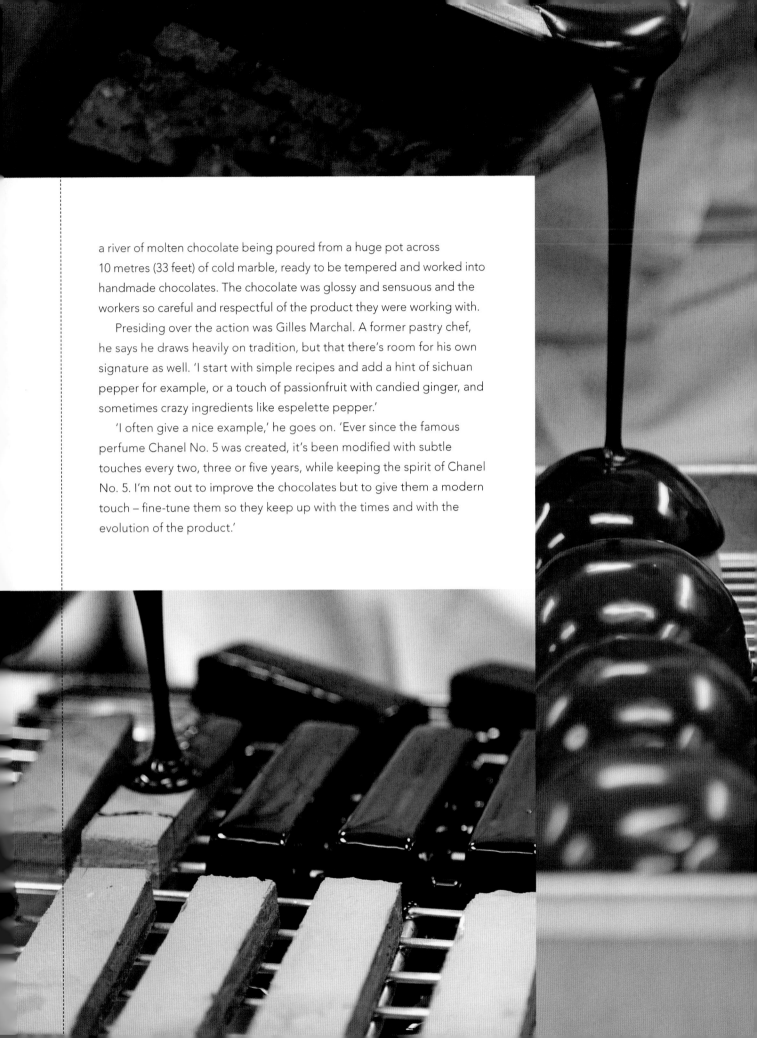

a river of molten chocolate being poured from a huge pot across 10 metres (33 feet) of cold marble, ready to be tempered and worked into handmade chocolates. The chocolate was glossy and sensuous and the workers so careful and respectful of the product they were working with.

Presiding over the action was Gilles Marchal. A former pastry chef, he says he draws heavily on tradition, but that there's room for his own signature as well. 'I start with simple recipes and add a hint of sichuan pepper for example, or a touch of passionfruit with candied ginger, and sometimes crazy ingredients like espelette pepper.'

'I often give a nice example,' he goes on. 'Ever since the famous perfume Chanel No. 5 was created, it's been modified with subtle touches every two, three or five years, while keeping the spirit of Chanel No. 5. I'm not out to improve the chocolates but to give them a modern touch – fine-tune them so they keep up with the times and with the evolution of the product.'

CHOCOLATE ALMOND MI-CUIT

from Pierrick Boyer

Serves 12

Cakes

250 g (9 oz) unsalted butter at room temperature, diced

200 g (7 oz) caster (superfine) sugar

300 g (10½ oz/3 cups) ground almonds, lightly roasted

40 g (1½ oz/⅓ cup) unsweetened cocoa powder

10 g (¼ oz) baking powder

5 eggs (50 g/1¾ oz each)

225 g (8 oz) dark couverture chocolate, finely chopped (leaving some larger pieces)

Chocolate streusel

125 g (4½ oz) unsalted butter at room temperature, diced

125 g (4½ oz) plain (all-purpose) flour

125 g (4½ oz) demerara sugar

90 g (3 oz) ground almonds

30 g (1 oz/¼ cup) unsweetened cocoa powder

½ teaspoon salt

Chantilly cream

300 ml (10 fl oz) pouring (single/light) cream

50 g (1¾ oz) caster sugar

1 tablespoon vanilla-bean paste

'Mi-cuit' translates as 'half-cooked', and in this case it refers to chocolate cake that is deliciously gooey and slightly molten on the inside, being purposely undercooked. Pierrick's version is served with vanilla chantilly cream and crunchy chocolate streusel, and he likes to decorate it with gold leaf and perfect large curls of tempered chocolate. It's artwork!

Preheat the oven to 175°C (350°F). Line 12 individual metal cake rings (about 4 cm/1½ in diameter and 5 cm/2 in high) with baking paper, extending the paper a couple of centimetres (just less than an inch) above the top of the rings. Place the rings on a tray.

Combine the butter, sugar, ground almonds, cocoa and baking powder in a bowl and mix until the butter is well combined (you can do this by hand with a spoon, or use an electric mixer with the paddle attachment). Mix in the eggs, then mix in the chocolate. Scoop into a piping bag and pipe into the cake rings, filling to a little below the top of the metal. Bake the cakes in the oven for 10–12 minutes.

While the cakes are in the oven, make the streusel. Combine the ingredients in a bowl and mix until fairly well combined but with the texture still rough and crumbly (you can rub the mixture between your fingers, or use an electric mixer with the paddle attachment). Scatter over a tray lined with baking paper and bake in the oven for 5–6 minutes.

To make the chantilly cream, combine the ingredients in a bowl and whip to stiff peaks.

To serve, remove the warm cakes from their rings and place on serving plates. Serve with the streusel and chantilly cream.

SALTED CARAMEL MACARONS

from Jean-Michel Raynaud

Makes 35–40 macarons

Macarons

300 g (10½ oz/3 cups) ground almonds

300 g (10½ oz) icing (confectioners') sugar

240 g (8½ oz) egg whites

300 g (10½ oz) white sugar

75 ml (2½ fl oz) water

a dash each of brown and yellow powdered food colouring

gold lustre dust

Salted caramel

250 ml (8½ fl oz/1 cup) pouring (single/light) cream

350 g (12½ oz) white sugar

350 g (12½ oz) chilled unsalted butter

10 g (¼ oz) sea salt

This is a recipe for the advanced cook, requiring sugar thermometers, piping bags and patience. The results are fabulous though ... nothing can match the joy in re-creating this patisserie item, which has been a hot seller in Australia for the past few years.

The basis of the macaron shells is Italian meringue – whipped egg whites with the addition of hot sugar syrup to form the glossiest, most stable meringue. Ground almonds are the other main ingredient. The emulsified caramel filling is sheer heaven, with the salt helping to reduce sweetness and also bitterness. As Jean-Michel explains: 'The caramel is cooked past the usual blonde and sweet mixture to a darker, reddish sugar, developing a much more complex flavour with hints of malt and wood. However, this comes with bitterness so we add salt to offset it and are left with a full-flavoured caramel that is not bitter and not too sweet.'

Combine the ground almonds, icing sugar and half the egg whites in a bowl and mix to a stiff batter. Set aside.

Combine the sugar, water, and brown and yellow colouring in a saucepan and place over high heat. Cook, stirring occasionally and scraping any sugar crystals from the sides of the pan, until the mixture reaches 120°C (248°F) on a sugar thermometer (this is firm-ball stage – when a small amount of syrup dropped into cold water can be rolled into a firm but pliable ball).

While the sugar is heating, put the remaining egg whites into the bowl of an electric mixer and whisk to stiff peaks – you should be able to dip your finger in and pull out a peak that will stand up, but make sure you don't over-mix the egg whites or they can split and give the macarons tiny air bubbles on top.

As soon as the sugar reaches temperature, and with the mixer on full speed, pour the hot sugar into the egg whites in a steady stream. Continue beating until the mixture cools to around 40°C (104°F). This should take around 3–4 minutes, and at the end you should have a thick, shiny, light brown meringue.

Gradually fold the meringue into the almond mixture to give a smooth and shiny batter. Transfer the mixture to a piping bag.

Preheat the oven to 155°C (310°F). Pipe rounds of about 4.5 cm (1¾ in) diameter onto trays lined with baking paper. Sprinkle the tops of the macarons with gold dust.

Bake the macarons in the oven for 10 minutes with the door slightly ajar to allow excess steam to escape (you could put a spoon in the door opening). Turn the oven down to 150°C (300°F) and bake for a further 12 minutes. When cooked, slide the baking paper and macarons onto a bench to cool.

To make the salted caramel, gently heat the cream in a small saucepan to boiling point. Meanwhile, put the sugar in another large saucepan without water and place over medium heat. Cook, stirring, until the sugar melts and then forms a dark caramel.

Gently pour the hot cream into the dark caramel with the saucepan still on the heat – be careful as the mixture will bubble up to twice its volume. Once incorporated, drop the butter into the caramel, stirring gently. Stop stirring and remove from the heat once the butter has melted but you can still see small streaks of butter through the caramel – this helps with emulsifying later. Pour the caramel into a bowl, cover with plastic wrap and cool in the refrigerator. Take it out once it reaches room temperature.

Whisk the caramel briskly, transforming it into a whipped, mayonnaise-like mixture. (If the caramel became too cold to whisk, you can set the bowl over a saucepan of simmering water and allow the mixture to warm slowly while you whisk it, but be careful not to heat and soften the caramel too much.) Whisk in the salt, and transfer the caramel to a piping bag.

Match macarons of similar size. Pipe a generous dollop of the caramel filling onto one macaron in each pair, and sandwich with the top macaron. Store the filled macarons in the refrigerator for at least 24 hours to let the macarons reabsorb some moisture and allow the flavour of the salt to develop in the filling.

VANILLA BEAN ICE-CREAM

from Guillaume Brahimi

Makes 1 litre (34 fl oz/4 cups)

375 ml (12½ fl oz/1½ cups) pouring (single/light) cream
375 ml (12½ fl oz/1½ cups) milk
2 vanilla pods, seeds scraped
150 g (5½ oz/⅔ cup) white sugar
8 egg yolks

This is the most luxurious and deeply satisfying ice-cream. Pastry-chef Kirsty Solomon from Guillaume at Bennelong says it is what many chefs would choose as their last taste on earth ... having tasted it, we know why!

Combine the cream, milk, vanilla seeds and scraped pods in a large saucepan and bring to a simmer.

Meanwhile, combine the sugar and egg yolks in a bowl and beat with electric beaters until pale and thick. Remove the beaters and gradually pour in the hot cream mixture, stirring until combined.

Return the mixture to the saucepan and cook over medium heat, stirring constantly, until thick enough to coat the back of the spoon. Strain the custard through a fine sieve into a bowl set over ice. Make sure you scrape all the vanilla seeds from the bottom of the sieve back into the custard. Leave the mixture to cool on the ice for a while, then chill in the refrigerator for 2 hours. Transfer to an ice-cream maker and churn according to the manufacturer's instructions.

If you don't have an ice-cream maker, you can freeze the bowl of mixture for 1½ hours. Remove from the freezer and stir well with a fork or beat with electric beaters, then return to the freezer. Repeat this every hour for another 3 hours or so (the more times you mix the ice-cream, the smoother and lighter the results). After the last mix, transfer the ice-cream to a container with a lid.

'IN ALL PROFESSIONS WITHOUT DOUBT, BUT CERTAINLY IN COOKING, ONE IS A STUDENT ALL HIS LIFE.'
Fernand Point, 20th century chef and restaurateur

CROQUEMBOUCHE

from Jean-François Perron

Sweet Shortcrust Pastry
(page 242)

Choux pastry

1 litre (34 fl oz/4 cups) water

400 g (14 oz) unsalted butter

1 tablespoon salt

600 g (1 lb 5 oz/4 cups) plain
(all-purpose) flour

16 eggs (50 g/1¾ oz each)

Crème pâtissière

1 litre (34 fl oz/4 cups) milk

250 g (9 oz) white sugar

1 vanilla pod, seeds scraped

50 g (1¾ oz) unsalted butter
(optional)

2 eggs plus 4 egg yolks

90–100 g (3–3½ oz) cornflour
(cornstarch), sifted

splash of Grand Marnier
or Cointreau

Toffee

1 kg (2 lb 3 oz) white sugar

330 ml (11 fl oz) water

200 g (7 oz) liquid glucose

pearl or hail sugar for
dipping (optional)

Croquembouche is perhaps the most spectacular creation to have come out of the world of French sweets – a towering sculpture of profiteroles filled with crème pâtissière, carefully constructed with toffee to seal it all together. The first croquembouche was said to have been created by legendary chef Antonin Carême in the shape of a Turkish fez – the conical shape evolved later. The confection can be decorated with spun sugar if desired, which sounds difficult but is in fact quite simple. If you wish to do this, multiply the toffee ingredients by 1.5 to make extra toffee.

Preheat the oven to 180°C (350°F). Roll out the shortcrust pastry and cut a circle 23 cm (9 in) in diameter. Place on a tray lined with baking paper and bake until lightly golden. Set aside to cool.

Turn the oven up to 210°C (410°F). Combine the water, butter and salt in a large saucepan and bring to the boil. Remove from the heat and stir in the flour. Return to the heat and stir constantly for around 3–4 minutes to allow some of the moisture to evaporate. Remove from the heat and transfer the dough to the bowl of an electric mixer fitted with the paddle attachment. Begin mixing, then gradually add the eggs (a few at a time) until well combined. Scoop the mixture into a piping bag.

Line more trays with baking paper and pipe the mixture onto the trays in rounds of 3 sizes – 3 cm, 4.5 cm and 6 cm (1¼ in, 1¾ in and 2½ in) – aiming for a roughly equal amount in each size. (This quantity of dough should make 70–100 rounds.) Bake in the oven for around 15 minutes, until puffed and golden, then turn the oven down to 170°C (340°F) and continue to cook for around 12 minutes more, to ensure the profiteroles are cooked through but without giving them any extra colour. Turn the oven off and leave the profiteroles inside with the door ajar for around 30 minutes. Then, transfer to a rack to cool.

To make the crème pâtissière, combine the milk, a quarter of the sugar, the vanilla seeds and butter (if using) in a large saucepan and heat gently until hot, then remove from the heat. Meanwhile, whisk the remaining sugar with the eggs and egg yolks in a large bowl until pale. Add the cornflour and a little of the hot milk and whisk well. Whisk this mixture into the hot milk and return the saucepan to medium heat, whisking constantly. Cook for around 3 minutes, until thick, smooth and glossy. Transfer to a clean bowl to cool.

Once cool, stir the liqueur into the custard and transfer to a piping bag fitted with a narrow nozzle. Use a sharp metal skewer to make a small hole in the base of each profiterole just large enough to fit the piping nozzle. Insert the nozzle into each profiterole and fill with custard.

To make the toffee, combine the sugar and water in a saucepan and bring to the boil. Once boiling, add the glucose. Continue to cook to a light golden brown (around 170°C/340°F on a sugar thermometer).

Carefully dip the top of each profiterole in toffee and place them toffee-side up on a tray lined with baking paper to cool briefly. If desired, you can dip some toffee-coated profiteroles in pearl sugar for an extra decorative touch.

To assemble the croquembouche, place the disc of shortcrust pastry on a work surface. Working from the largest profiteroles to the smallest, begin to dip their bases in toffee one by one and form a circle around the rim of the pastry, sticking down with the toffee. Drizzle the layer with a little toffee and continue to dip more profiteroles and build another layer. Continue to build the profiterole tower, allowing the walls to lean slightly inwards in order to meet in a peak at the top. If you dipped some profiteroles in pearl sugar, scatter these randomly in the tower.

If you wish to decorate the tower with spun sugar and have extra toffee, dip a fork into the remaining toffee, coating it well, then hold it above the tower and flick it carefully but rapidly from side to side, which should coat the tower in long delicate strands of toffee. Continue to dip the fork and flick the sugar until the tower is coated in a cocoon of spun sugar. Carefully lift the finished croquembouche onto a serving plate.

MILLE-FEUILLE

from Pierre Charkos

Puff Pastry (page 241)
Crème Pâtissière (page 257)
icing (confectioners') sugar to dust

This recipe from late Sydney pâtissier Pierre Charkos, who founded La Renaissance Patisserie in 1974, remains a favourite with customers. Layers of light pastry wafers are sandwiched with rich custard – the French version of vanilla slice, but so much more luxurious with proper crème pâtissière and handmade butter puff pastry.

Preheat the oven to 200°C (400°F). Place the pastry on a lightly floured work surface and roll out to about 3 mm (⅛ in) thick. Use a scone cutter to cut 3 circles of pastry for each mille-feuille, making as many mille-feuille as desired. (If you have a cutter with a fluted edge, then this makes for especially pretty mille-feuille.)

Place the circles on trays lined with baking paper and bake in the oven for around 20 minutes, until puffed and golden. Leave to cool.

To assemble the mille-feuille, start with a circle of pastry as the base. Spoon on a generous amount of crème pâtissière. Add another circle of pastry and spoon on more crème pâtissière. Top with another circle of pastry. Dust the top with icing sugar.

FRENCH KITCHEN

FRENCH KITCHEN

It's almost midday in the huge kitchen in the basement of luxurious Paris hotel the Plaza Athénée, and it's as though an electric current has suddenly galvanised the chefs who are scrubbing down benches getting ready for lunch service. The level of action in Alain Ducasse's kitchen seems to get faster as the minutes tick by.

The chefs have diced and peeled and braised and sautéed all morning – and when those first orders start coming through, another new burst of energy hits the kitchen. Orders are rapidly called out and there is a chorus of 'oui chef' as each station gets to work. As an observer you feel your heart beat faster when service hits its busiest time – a sensory overload of sound, smell and action.

Each member of the team of any great kitchen strives for excellence in every dish, and it's intriguing to learn that the chain of command – the pecking order of staff – was borrowed from the military.

Chef Auguste Escoffier devised the hierarchy of the kitchen after spending time in the French army and recognising how smoothly everything worked when there was one commander and a number of deputies who knew their jobs and carried them out. He decided that the kitchen should be divided into sections and personnel that would each concentrate on a type of food or cooking – the *saucier* for the all-important sauces, *poissonnier* for fish, *grillardin* for grills, *friturier* for fried foods, *rôtisseur* for roasts, *garde manger* for cold larder, *legumier* for vegetables and pâtissier for pastries. At the top of the pyramid is the *chef de cuisine* – the executive chef – followed by their deputy, the sous chef.

If you haven't had the opportunity to watch a French kitchen in action, the charming animated film *Ratatouille* is actually a great example of a working kitchen, modelled on that of Alain Ducasse. You also get a sense of the hard slog and determination it takes to start out as an apprentice and work your way up. The French system is demanding, but that's what helps to make the food taste so wonderful. In top kitchens there is no room for second best.

'It's like a wheel,' explains Guillaume Brahimi. 'If you're not up to scratch the wheel will spin you out. As executive chef it's ultimately up to me, but if in the body of the kitchen someone isn't up to doing the work, the others will be onto it … Teamwork is everything in the kitchen.'

Like many other chefs we spent time with, Guillaume was keen to make the point that 'you are only as good as your last meal'. 'Your expectations of yourself

must be high and as captain of the ship you need to lead by example … You need to keep the standards high,' he says.

The pursuit of excellence in France (and now in Europe and major cities in America and Asia) is recognised by the Michelin star system, which rates the top restaurants. To have three stars is an unparalleled honour, awarded to just over twenty restaurants in France. By comparison, there are several hundred restaurants recognised as one star across the country.

The Michelin system was created by two enterprising brothers who made tyres. In 1900 they published a guide to alert car owners and chauffeurs to where they could find fuel, recharge batteries and, if necessary, change tyres. At that time there were around three thousand cars in all of France and the guide was indispensable in helping drivers negotiate rough and often unmarked roads. It was a free booklet until 1920, and a list of hotels and restaurants was added in 1923. The star system was introduced three years later.

In Guillaume's kitchen at Guillaume at Bennelong, the action has a similar crescendo to what we experienced at the Plaza Athénée. The team works to create magic for hundreds of diners at the Sydney Opera House every service. The work is precise and intense, but as one young chef told us: 'Well, you don't want to have a boring job – you want to be doing something you like doing … When the chef calls the orders we all switch on.'

I'll leave the last word on the French kitchen to renowned chef Guy Savoy, who has Michelin-starred restaurants in France, Singapore and the United States. He says he loves using the best produce from what he calls 'the craftsmen of the land and the sea'. 'I stay fifteen hours every day in this place. If I don't love it then it's impossible to do. I love my team and I love my guests. And I love life!'

'TASTING A DISH SHOULD BE MEMORABLE …
IF NOTHING REMAINS IN THE MEMORY OF A
SINGLE GUEST, THEN I HAVE MADE A MISTAKE.'
Alain Ducasse

PUFF PASTRY

from Jean-Michel Raynaud and Pierre Charkos

Makes 1.1 kg (2 lb 7 oz)

500 g (1 lb 2 oz/3⅓ cups) plain (all-purpose) flour

50 g (1¾ oz) unsalted butter at room temperature, plus 350 g (12½ oz) chilled unsalted butter

1½ teaspoons salt

250 ml (8½ fl oz/1 cup) ice-cold water

Making puff pastry is not as hard as you might imagine – you could think of the process as therapeutic, and the results are very satisfying. However, if you would prefer to make Rough Puff Pastry instead, see the recipe on page 242.

Mound the flour on a work surface and make a well in the centre. Dice the room-temperature butter and scatter it over the flour along with the salt. Pour some of the water into the well and start mixing the water and butter into the flour with your hands. Keep adding the rest of the water and mixing until you form a firm dough. Shape into a ball, cover with plastic wrap and chill in the refrigerator for 30 minutes. At the same time as you put the pastry in the refrigerator, get the chilled butter out of the refrigerator to soften slightly.

After 25 minutes or so, put this butter between 2 sheets of plastic wrap and flatten with a rolling pin to a book shape.

Unwrap the dough and place on a lightly floured surface. Cut a cross in the top of the dough going about halfway down. Pull out each corner of the cross, then roll out to flatten the cross. Put the slab of butter in the middle of the cross, then fold the sides of the cross over the butter.

Roll the slab of pastry away from you into a long rectangle. Fold in the ends to meet in the middle, then fold in half to make a book shape. Turn the book so a short edge is facing you and roll out again to a long rectangle. Repeat the folds. Cover the pastry book in plastic wrap and chill in the refrigerator for 30 minutes.

Repeat another set of rolls and folds (2 of each) and chill for another 30 minutes. Repeat again. After chilling for a final 30 minutes the pastry is ready to use. If you don't need to use all the pastry at once, it can be frozen.

'METTRE LA MAIN À LA PÂTE.'

(To get to work; put your hand to the dough.)

ROUGH PUFF PASTRY

from Guillaume Brahimi

Makes 1.25 kg (2 lb 12 oz)

500 g (1 lb 2 oz/3⅓ cups) plain (all-purpose) flour

500 g (1 lb 2 oz) chilled unsalted butter, diced

1½ teaspoons salt

250 ml (8½ fl oz/1 cup) iced water

This easier puff pastry rises almost as much as the classic puff pastry (page 241). The main difference lies in how the butter is incorporated – in true puff pastry it is added as a layer with the pastry folded around it. Each time the pastry is rolled and folded again, the layers of butter multiply and get thinner and thinner. In rough puff pastry, the butter is combined with the flour at the beginning.

Mound the flour on a work surface and make a well in the centre. Add the butter and salt to the well and use your fingertips to gradually rub the flour into the butter. When the butter is in small pieces, giving the flour a grainy texture, gradually add the water. Mix until just incorporated into a dough. Shape into a disc and cover in plastic wrap. Chill in the refrigerator for 20 minutes.

Place the pastry on a lightly floured work surface and roll it away from you into a long rectangle, about 20 x 40 cm (8 x 16 in). Fold in one of the ends, going two-thirds of the way to the other end. Fold the other end on top, giving a stack of three layers like a folded pamphlet. Turn the stack so a short edge is facing you and roll out to another long rectangle, then fold into three again. Cover in plastic wrap and chill for another 30 minutes.

Repeat another set of rolls and folds (2 of each) and chill for another 30 minutes. The pastry is now ready to use. If you don't need to use all the pastry at once, it can be frozen.

PÂTE SUCRÉE

SWEET SHORTCRUST PASTRY

from Jean-Michel Raynaud and Pierre Charkos

Makes 1 x 26 cm (10½ in) tart or 6–8 individual tarts

100 g (3½ oz) unsalted butter at room temperature

100 g (3½ oz) caster (superfine) sugar

1 egg

200 g (7 oz/1⅓ cups) plain (all-purpose) flour

This is the pastry for desserts, tarts and sweet pies. It can be made ahead of time and frozen until needed.

Combine the butter and sugar in a bowl and mix thoroughly. Stir in the egg. Sift the flour on top and mix until combined. Press the dough together and knead very briefly. Shape into a disc, cover in plastic wrap and chill in the refrigerator for 1–2 hours before using.

PÂTE À CHOUX

CHOUX PASTRY

from Guillaume Brahimi

Makes 30–40 profiteroles

150 ml (5 fl oz) milk

150 ml (5 fl oz) water

120 g (4½ oz) unsalted butter, diced

½ teaspoon salt

150 g (5½ oz/1 cup) plain (all-purpose) flour

4 eggs, plus 1 for the egg wash

This beautifully light pastry is used to make profiteroles and eclairs, and is quite easy to make. It's a twice-cooked pastry as the dough of milk, water, butter and flour is cooked on the stove. Then the eggs are added and the pastry is complete, ready for piping and baking.

Combine the milk, water, butter and salt in a medium saucepan and place over low heat. Slowly bring to the boil, stirring until the butter dissolves.

Remove the pan from the heat and sift in the flour, stirring to a smooth paste. Return the pan to medium heat and cook, stirring constantly, for about 1 minute, until a ball of dough is formed.

Transfer the dough to a bowl and leave to cool for 5 minutes. Lightly beat the eggs in a separate bowl, then gradually stir the eggs into the dough, making sure each addition is absorbed before adding the next. The dough should now be a smooth and shiny paste.

To bake profiteroles or eclairs, preheat the oven to 210°C (410°F) and line a tray with baking paper. To make ball shapes for profiteroles, use a piping bag or 2 spoons – take a spoon of mixture and scoop it onto the tray with the second spoon. To make log shapes for eclairs, it is easiest to use a piping bag. Leave at least 3 cm (1¼ in) between your shapes on the tray to allow for expansion during baking. Lightly beat the egg for the egg wash and brush it over the surface of the shapes. Bake for about 6–7 minutes, until risen, then reduce the temperature to 170°C (340°F) and continue to bake for another 3–4 minutes, until golden and crisp.

FLAVOURED (COMPOUND) BUTTERS

from Guillaume Brahimi

Maître d'hôtel butter

300 g (10½ oz) unsalted butter at room temperature

¼ bunch flat-leaf (Italian) parsley, finely chopped

4 chives, finely chopped

¼ garlic clove, crushed

juice of ¼ lemon

sea salt and freshly ground black pepper

Anchovy butter

50 g (1¾ oz) anchovy fillets, well drained

250 g (9 oz) unsalted butter at room temperature

lemon juice

freshly ground black pepper

Tarragon butter

250 g (9 oz) unsalted butter at room temperature

½ cup tarragon leaves, finely chopped

1 small garlic clove, crushed

sea salt and freshly ground black pepper

Red wine and shallot butter

250 ml (8½ fl oz/1 cup) red wine

1 French shallot, finely chopped

2 tablespoons Chicken Stock (page 250)

200 g (7 oz) unsalted butter at room temperature

1 tablespoon finely chopped flat-leaf (Italian) parsley

lemon juice

sea salt and freshly ground black pepper

It's such a simple idea, adding aromatic ingredients to butter, but it makes a superb all-purpose sauce that you can quickly whip from your fridge or freezer whenever you need it.

Once you've blended the butter, scoop it onto a sheet of baking paper and shape into a thick sausage using the paper. Roll the sausage up inside the paper and twist the ends to seal shut, then refrigerate until firm.

You can keep the butter for a week or so in the refrigerator – just wrap the paper in an extra layer of plastic wrap so it's airtight. To serve the butter, slice it into 5 mm (¼ in) discs. Alternatively, pre-slice the butter and store the portions separated by layers of baking paper in a container in the freezer.

MAÎTRE D'HÔTEL BUTTER

This classic blend includes parsley, chives, garlic and lemon zest and is perfect with grilled meat or fish.

Mix all the ingredients together until well combined, adding salt and pepper to taste.

ANCHOVY BUTTER

Anchovy butter is fantastic served with steak as an alternative to maître d'hôtel butter, and is also good with grilled fish.

Mash the anchovies to a paste in a mortar. Transfer to a bowl (or use the mortar if it is large enough) and stir in the butter, as well as lemon juice and pepper to taste.

TARRAGON BUTTER

Tarragon butter is delicious with chicken – try basting a roast chicken with it as it cooks. The butter is also a good match for seared scallops.

Mix all the ingredients together until well combined, adding salt and pepper to taste.

RED WINE AND SHALLOT BUTTER

With a rich red-wine flavour, it's another butter to serve with a steak, or even grilled salmon.

Combine the red wine, shallot and chicken stock in a small saucepan and bring to a rolling boil. Cook until the liquid reduces by three-quarters, then set aside to cool.

Mix the wine and shallot mixture with the remaining ingredients, adding lemon juice, salt and pepper to taste.

Sauces

Sauces are essential to the food equation in France, used since the Middle Ages to add flavour, moisture and visual appeal to a dish. Mastering sauces is one of the earliest lessons for a chef and one of the most crucial roles in the commercial kitchen. Chef and restaurateur Fernand Point once said: 'In the orchestra of a great kitchen, the sauce chef is the soloist.'

Sydney chef Tony Bilson, whose life's work of over forty years has been the pursuit of excellence in gastronomy, particularly French gastronomy, considers sauces 'the bridge between the main ingredients and the palate if you like … They provide the sense of finesse. They provide the seasoning. But they also provide links to the wines and things that you're drinking with the food at the same time.'

There are hundreds of French sauces based on ingredients such as stock, butter, eggs, milk, cream or wine. Nineteenth-century chef Antonin Câreme was responsible for developing and classifying many sauces and creating a list of four *grandes sauces* ('mother sauces'). In the early twentieth century Auguste Escoffier revised the list from four mother sauces to five, which are still considered the basic French sauces today. They are:

Espagnole: A brown sauce of roasted veal stock beginning with a well-coloured roux.
Bechamel: A milk-based sauce beginning with a briefly cooked blonde roux.
Velouté: A sauce of white (unroasted) stock beginning with a briefly cooked blonde roux.
Tomato: Tomato sauce, again classically thickened with roux.
Hollandaise: Sauce of egg yolks and butter flavoured with lemon juice, vinegar or both, thickened by adding the butter gradually and whisking to create an emulsion.

The French countryside has contributed key ingredients to the country's sauces, such as the cream in *sauce Normande*; fresh butter in *beurre blanc*; garlic in aioli; mustard in *sauce Dijonnaise*; red wine in *sauce Bordelaise*; and onions in *sauce Lyonnaise*.

CHICKEN STOCK

from Guillaume Brahimi

Makes 2 litres (68 fl oz/8 cups)

2 kg (4 lb 6 oz) chicken carcasses or bones (without skin)

1 onion, diced

1 carrot, diced

1 celery stalk, diced

½ garlic bulb, sliced in half through the cloves

¼ bunch thyme

1 bay leaf

freshly ground black pepper

4 litres (135 fl oz/16 cups) water

This is one of the key building blocks of the French kitchen, made every day and put to use in soups, sauces and stews. Some chefs boil the bones and vegetables for many hours, but Guillaume believes the stock doesn't need to be too heavy and an hour is enough to extract the flavour needed.

Combine the ingredients in a large pot. Bring to the boil, skimming the surface of foam and impurities. Reduce the heat to a simmer and cook, skimming occasionally, for 1 hour. Remove from the heat and leave to rest for 20 minutes before straining through a fine sieve without pressing down on the bones (which could make the stock cloudy). Chill in the refrigerator. Once cold, spoon any fat from the surface. Store in the refrigerator for up to 3 days or freeze for up to 1 month.

FISH STOCK

from Guillaume Brahimi

heads and bones of 3 snapper (porgy)

2 leeks, diced

1 carrot, diced

3 celery stalks, diced

1 onion, diced

3 French shallots, diced

stems from ½ bunch parsley, chopped

3 bay leaves

handful of thyme sprigs

10 white peppercorns

water

Fish stock is cooked for just a short period of time, as lengthy cooking can make it bitter. It makes a light yet flavoursome base for soups and stews including Bouillabaisse (page 171), an intense celebration of the sea.

Place the ingredients in a large pot, adding water to cover generously. Bring to the boil, skimming the surface of foam and impurities. Reduce the heat to a simmer and cook, skimming occasionally, for 20 minutes. Leave to cool for a further 20 minutes before straining through a fine sieve without pressing down on the bones (which could make the stock cloudy). Chill and store in the refrigerator for up to 3 days, or freeze for up to 1 month.

VEAL (OR BEEF) STOCK AND JUS

from Guillaume Brahimi

Makes 2 litres (68 fl oz/8 cups) stock
or 650 ml (22 fl oz) jus

2 tablespoons vegetable oil

2 kg (4 lb 6 oz) veal (or beef) osso bucco

1 onion, diced

1 carrot, diced

1 celery stalk, diced

2 tomatoes, diced (for jus only)

½ garlic bulb, sliced in half through the cloves

¼ bunch thyme

1 bay leaf

freshly ground black pepper

4 litres (135 fl oz/16 cups) water

Veal stock is used regularly in the French kitchen. The bones of veal are high in collagen, which gives a velvety, viscous texture, particularly when making concentrated stock called jus that is used to enrich many sauces and dishes.

Please note that you can also use this recipe to make beef stock using beef osso bucco. In addition, you can make a delicious chicken jus if you substitute chicken wings for the veal.

Heat half the oil in a large pot over high heat. When hot, add half the veal (or beef) pieces and fry on each side until well browned. Transfer to a plate and brown the remaining veal in the remaining oil. Remove to the plate and add the onion, carrot, celery, tomato (if making jus) and garlic to the pot. Cook, stirring occasionally, for another 6–8 minutes, until the vegetables are coloured and starting to soften. Return the veal to the pot and add the herbs, some pepper and the water and bring to the boil, skimming the surface of foam and impurities.

Reduce the heat to a simmer and continue to skim occasionally. If making stock, simmer for 4 hours and top up with water as needed to keep the veal covered (but let the water partly reduce). If making jus, simmer without adding extra water until reduced to around 650 ml (22 fl oz).

Strain the stock or jus through a fine sieve and chill in the refrigerator. Once cold, spoon any fat from the surface. Store in the refrigerator for up to 3 days or freeze for up to 1 month.

'NE PAS SAVOIR À QUELLE SAUCE ON VA ÊTRE MANGE.'
(Uncertain fate; not knowing what sauce you're going to be eaten with.)

SAUCE CHASSEUR

HUNTER'S SAUCE

from Guillaume Brahimi

Serves 4

400 ml (13½ fl oz) Chicken Stock
(page 250)

1 roma (plum) tomato

40 g (1½ oz) unsalted butter

6 Swiss brown mushrooms,
stems removed, sliced

1 French shallot, finely chopped

75 ml (2½ fl oz) dry white wine

1 small tarragon sprig, leaves
picked

freshly ground white pepper

This brown sauce is a rich blend of mushrooms, shallots and white wine, and sometimes tomato and parsley. It's perfect served with game and other meats (the catch of the hunter).

Pour the chicken stock into a saucepan and boil until reduced by a little over half.

Make a cut in the base of the tomato and drop it into a bowl of hot water for 30 seconds. Remove from the water and peel off the skin. Cut the tomato in half and remove the core and seeds. Finely dice the flesh.

Melt the butter in a heavy-based saucepan over medium heat. Add the mushrooms and sauté for 3 minutes, then add the shallot and sauté for another 2–3 minutes. Stir through the diced tomato and pour in the wine, deglazing the bottom of the pan. Simmer until the wine reduces by half. Pour in the reduced chicken stock and simmer until reduced by another third. Remove from the heat and stir through the tarragon and white pepper to taste.

SAUCE BORDELAISE

RED-WINE SAUCE

from Guillaume Brahimi

Serves 2

40 g (1½ oz) unsalted butter

1 medium onion, finely chopped

1 garlic clove, finely chopped

125 ml (4 fl oz/½ cup) dry red wine

250 ml (8½ fl oz/1 cup) Beef Stock
(page 253)

freshly ground black pepper

Named after Bordeaux, the wine region of France, this hearty sauce is based on red wine and stock. It's a common feature on French-inspired menus worldwide, and can add sophisticated flavour to a wide variety of dishes, particularly meat.

Melt the butter in a frying pan over medium heat. Add the onion and sauté for 3–4 minutes, until softened, then add the garlic and cook for a minute more, until fragrant. Pour in the wine and simmer for 3–5 minutes. Pour in the stock and simmer for 10–12 minutes, or until thickened. Season with pepper to taste.

CRÈME PÂTISSIÈRE

from Jean-Michel Raynaud and Pierre Charkos

Makes about 700 ml (23½ fl oz)

500 ml (17 fl oz/2 cups) milk

½ vanilla pod, seeds scraped

4 egg yolks

125 g (4½ oz) caster (superfine) sugar

40 g (1½ oz/⅓ cup) cornflour (cornstarch), sifted

75 g (2¾ oz) unsalted butter

This deliciously rich egg custard serves many purposes in the French patisserie. It is piped into profiteroles and eclairs, used as a filling in tarts and cakes, and layered between sheets of puff pastry to make Mille-Feuille (page 233).

Combine the milk and vanilla seeds in a large saucepan and bring to a simmer.

Whisk the egg yolks and sugar in a large bowl until pale, then whisk in the cornflour. Once the milk is simmering, pour half of it over the egg mixture, whisking well. Return the mixture back to the remaining milk in the saucepan and place over medium heat. Cook, stirring constantly, until thick and smooth. Stir in the butter and remove from the heat, and allow to cool before using.

MAYONNAISE

from Guillaume Brahimi

Makes 350–450 ml (12–15 fl oz)

2 egg yolks

1 teaspoon dijon mustard

pinch of sea salt

pinch of freshly ground white pepper

300–400 ml (10–13½ fl oz) grapeseed oil

a little white-wine vinegar or lemon juice

You'll never buy mayonnaise again when you know how delicious it can be, and how simple it is to make. French chefs whip this up using a whisk, but if this sounds daunting to you a food processor is quite acceptable.

Sit a large mixing bowl on a folded damp cloth to keep it stable. Add the egg yolks, mustard, salt and pepper to the bowl and whisk well.

Start adding the oil, just a few drops to start with, whisking constantly. (Making rapid figure-eights is an effective way to whisk.) Keep adding small amounts of oil and whisking well after each addition. The mayonnaise should begin to thicken once about 60–80 ml (2–2½ fl oz/¼–⅓ cup) of oil has been added. Then you can start adding the oil in a thin and steady stream down the side of the bowl while you continue whisking. Stop adding oil once you have reached the desired thickness, but whisk the mayonnaise for another minute until nicely glossy. Whisk in vinegar or lemon juice to taste and check the seasoning. If you would prefer your mayonnaise a little thinner, you can whisk in a little warm water.

Mayonnaise can be stored in the refrigerator for up to 1 week.

ACKNOWLEDGEMENTS

This beautiful book is the result of the passion and hard work of many people who have contributed their skills, recipes and time.

To the driving force behind the television series and books – my partner, talented Francophile Toufic Charabati, whose love and respect for the intricacies of French cuisine are apparent in every frame. Getting the series right and making it sing from the screen have laid a solid basis for this book. It's been so much fun to share the journey, and buy blowtorches, ramekins, crepe pans and whisks to recreate so many great recipes at home.

To Guillaume Brahimi, who opened his home so we could film recipes for *French Food Safari* (assisted by chef Graeme McLaughlin, who helped with preparation and kept a record of the precious recipes; thanks also to Guillaume's wife Sanchia). Thanks as well to the dedicated team at Guillaume at Bennelong who were very tolerant of the television invasion. Special thanks to pastry queen Kirsty Solomon.

We were blessed to have Guillaume guiding us in our travels – what better person to lead us through France than a chef both knowledgeable and passionate about the food of his homeland, and with connections that opened doors to some of the top producers, providores and restaurateurs. Thanks also to Guillaume's unflappable right-hand Aisha Cooper, who juggles his impossible schedule.

Another Francophile, Georgie Neal, has been crucial in every part of research for the television series and fact checking for this book, staying up late at night to speak in perfect French to our connections throughout France, and accompanying us on the trip. She led us to ingredients, talented chefs, pâtissiers and bakers; unearthed snippets of wisdom; and checked and rechecked everything in English and French. *Merci beaucoup* Georgie!

Also big thanks to the wonderful Jacinta Dunn who was fundamental in making our filming such a success, from sounding out story ideas, to logistics and the thousand things that are incredibly urgent in the behind the scenes of the production office … and to our great editor 'Coco' Kerry Anne Wallach who made the pictures sing; and to Peter Clarke who filmed them. And to the calm oasis that is Suzy Brien who runs Gourmet Safaris so smoothly while tornados of television work whip around her.

Thanks to Tonton Frank O'Meara, my dear uncle who lives in France and helped with many of the wisdom quotes in this book, as well as my knowledge and understanding of his adopted home.

A huge thanks to the team at SBS, including Sharon Ramsay-Luck – you're the godmother of this third beautiful *Food Safari* book; our commissioning editor Erik Dwyer, who said all the right things at the right times and got hungry with us as the series was coming together; and the SBS management for continuing to support *Food Safari* and allowing us to delve into the best of France.

To the wonderful cooks and chefs who so generously shared their wisdom and tried and true recipes and allowed us into their realm – to chef and cookbook writer Stéphane Reynaud and his family Isabelle, Jean, Basile and Zoë who so kindly welcomed us into their home and their lives; their friend Marcel; to two angels behind the scenes who helped doors to open – in Paris, Wendy Lyn and in Périgord, Trish Hobbs.

Sincere thanks to renowned chefs Alain Ducasse, Paul Bocuse, Guy Savoy, Shannon Bennett, Jacques Reymond, Philippe Mouchel, Robert Molines, Damien Pignolet, Dany Chouet, France Vidal, Serge Dansereau, Peter Robinson, Warren Turnbull, Michael Smith, Meyjitte Boughenout, Robert Molines, Christophe Saintaigne, Gabriel Gaté, Laurent Branover, Chui Lee Luk, Kirsty Solomon, Yves Camdeborde and Tony Bilson.

Thanks to the creators of sweet dreams – pâtissiers Pierre Hermé, Jean-Michel Raynaud and the late Pierre Charkos, Fabrice Le Bourdat, Pierrick Boyer, Vincent Gadan, Jean-François Perron and chocolate magician Gilles Marchal.

Thanks to charcutiers Romeo Baudouin and Stéphane Teyssier, wine writer Ben Edwards, truffle king Pierre-Jean Pebeyre and his family, butter expert Jean-Yves Bordier, poultry farmers Christian and Véronqiue Picard, cheese guru Will Studd, bakers Jean-Luc Poujauran and Apollonia Poilane, stylist Marie-Hélène Clauzon, affineur Laurent Dubois, restaurateur Yves Rivoiron; and to Mumm Champagne and their chief winemaker Didier Mariotti.

To the team at Hardie Grant – special thanks to publisher Pam Brewster, who added her considerable wisdom on all things French to the book and oversaw every aspect of its production, and to the detailed eye of editor Rachel Pitts for helping us get it right and suggesting ways to make it better. A wonderful job! Also thanks to those behind the scenes, stylist Simon Bajada, designer Hamish Freeman and photographer Gorta Yuuki.

Final thanks to my dear mum who has encouraged me and believed in me for so long and to the young team at home – Conor, Kitty and Scarlett; Francophiles all, food lovers and keen explorers of new delicious tastes – so good you're learning about the important things in life: food, togetherness and family.

INDEX TO RECIPES

Crique Ardéchois (page 10) from *365 good reasons to sit down and eat* by Stéphane Reynaud first published by Hachette Livre/Marabout published in English by Murdoch Books. Reprinted with permission of Hachette Livre/Marabout.

Pissaladière (page 22) from Philippe Mouchel in *Taste le Tour* by Gabriel Gaté published by Hardie Grant Books.

Autumn and winter vegetables and fruits en cocotte (page 61) from *Nature* by Alain Duccasse published in English by Hardie Grant Books and first published by Les Éditions Culinaires. Reprinted with permission of Alain Ducasse Groupe.

Caramelised pork belly (page 115) from *365 good reasons to sit down and eat* by Stéphane Reynaud first published by Hachette Livre/Marabout published in English by Murdoch Books. Reprinted with permission of Hachette Livre/Marabout.

Salade Nicoise (page 119) from *Salades* by Damien Pignolet published by Lantern, Penguin Books Australia.

Boufe en Croûte (page 160) from *French Kitchen* by Serge Dansereau published by ABC Books.

Fish Quenelles (page 194) from Philippe Mouchel in *Taste le Tour* by Gabriel Gaté published by Hardie Grant Books.

An SBS Book

This edition published in 2013
First published in 2012 by Hardie Grant Books

Hardie Grant Books (Australia)
Ground Floor, Building 1
658 Church Street
Richmond, Victoria 3121
www.hardiegrant.com.au

Hardie Grant Books (UK)
Dudley House, North Suite
34–35 Southampton Street
London WC2E 7HF
www.hardiegrant.co.uk

Cataloguing-in-Publication data is available from the National Library of Australia.

French Food Safari
ISBN: 9781742706917

Publisher: Pam Brewster
Cover and text design: Pfisterer + Freeman
Studio food photography: Gorta Yuuki
Additional studio photography: Joe Ashton, Omid photography
Food stylist: Simon Bajada
Location photography: Toufic Charabati
Photography in France: Oliver Strewe, Gorta Yuuki.
Food preparation team: Michael Smith (chef), Orlando Artavilla (pastry chef), Toula Ploumidis, Peta Grey, Emma Christian
Cover portrait of Maeve O'Meara and Guillaume Brahimi: Peter Collie
Portrait of Pierre Hermé: Jean-Louis Bloch Lain
Photographs of Pierre Hermés food: Pierre Hermé Paris
Portrait of Warren Turnbull: Dominique Cherry and Heath Bennett

The publishers would like to thank the following for their generosity in supplying props for the book: Mud ceramics, The Works, Bed Bath and Table and Izzi & Popo.

Colour reproduction by Splitting Image Colour Studio
Printed in China by 1010 Printing International Limited